The Physician Leader's Guide to Affiliation Options: Economics, Tactics, and Real-World Implementation

Max Reiboldt, CPA
Acuvance Coker

AAPL

978-1-960762-59-7 print
978-1-960762-60-3 eBook

Published by **American Association for Physician Leadership, Inc.**
PO Box 96503 | BMB 97493 | Washington, DC 20090-6503

Website: www.physicianleaders.org

13 8 7 6 5 4 3 2 1

Copyedited, typeset, indexed, and printed in the United States of America

PUBLISHER
Nancy Collins

PRODUCTION MANAGER
Jennifer Weiss

DESIGN & LAYOUT
Carter Publishing Studio

COPYEDITOR
Patricia George

Acknowledgments

WE APPRECIATE THE OPPORTUNITY to work with Nancy Collins, senior vice president of the American Association for Physician Leadership, to publish *The Physician Leader's Guide to Affiliation Options: Economics, Tactics, and Real-World Implementation.* With her loyal support, the advisers at Acuvance Coker have delivered vital information to the AAPL membership to fill the gap on the various affiliation options in the ever-changing healthcare business. Thank you, Nancy, for recognizing the necessity for this information.

We also thank Chad Eckhardt, attorney at law, Frost Brown Todd LLP, for his contributions to numerous legal aspects of affiliation transactions. His experience in such deals equips him as an ideal resource for this book. Thank you, Chad.

Table of Contents

About the Authors

Max Reiboldt, CPA, is the chairperson of Acuvance Coker. As chairperson, he occupies a senior executive role and contributes as a member of the firm's board. He has a passion for collaborating with clients and organizations of all sizes, engaging in consulting projects nationwide.

For more than 40 years, Reiboldt has provided invaluable experience working in business and industry, primarily involving healthcare providers. He contributes strategic, tactical, financial, and management expertise that health systems, physicians, and other healthcare entities and/or investors require in today's evolving marketplace.

Reiboldt understands the nuances of the healthcare industry, especially in such a dynamic age. He recognizes that healthcare organizations must maintain viability in a highly competitive market. Whether a transitional provider or a more trailblazing healthcare entity, Reiboldt works with organizations to provide sound solutions to daily and long-range challenges. Clients value his hands-on approach, open communication skills, and responsiveness. Transactional-related initiatives are no exception as he has assisted in hundreds of affiliation negotiations and strategic/tactical assignments related to this broad topic. This experience uniquely qualifies him to contribute to *The Physician Leader's Guide to Affiliation Options: Economics, Tactics, and Real-World Implementation.*

Contact Reiboldt at mreiboldt@cokergroup.com.

Mark Reiboldt is executive vice president and director of strategy at Acuvance Coker, where he specializes in financial and transaction advisory for hospitals, medical groups, and other healthcare organizations. These transactions include mergers and acquisitions, divestitures, equity purchases, physician alignment deals, and joint ventures.

Reiboldt's advisory services often entail acquisition/investment due diligence, valuation services, transaction management, buy-side representation, strategic alternatives processes, and post-merger integration. He serves on the executive leadership team and collaborates with the firm's senior management on various strategic projects. He is a board member of the Coker Foundation, the firm's nonprofit charity organization. Contact him at markreiboldt@cokergroup.com.

Chad N. Eckhardt is an attorney with Frost Brown Todd LLC and leads the firm's Health Care Innovation Industry Team. With a focus on the healthcare industry, he advises businesses and healthcare entities on corporate matters, formation and structuring, contract negotiation, and regulatory compliance. He works with publicly traded and privately owned healthcare entities, including many not-for-profit organizations.

Eckhardt has assisted many hospitals, physician practices, ancillary service providers, and related entities on mergers, acquisitions, and clinical integrations and issues pertaining to Stark, anti-kickback, billing compliance, recovery auditor programs, HIPAA, licensing, healthcare reform, and other regulatory and transactional aspects of the industry. He also advises not-for-profit organizations on governance and policy issues, IRS compliance, and Form 990 issues.

Prior to graduating from Salmon P. Chase College of Law, he taught English at the secondary and collegiate levels. Contact him at ceckhardt@fbtlaw.com.

Armani Cato, MBA, is a senior associate at Acuvance Coker. Cato has more than eight years of experience in the financial and professional services industry, specializing in capital markets, financial analysis, due diligence, commercial real estate, accounting, and client management. His work has involved assisting clients with audits, valuations, project feasibility, real property appraisals, and providing investment advice to a high-net-worth client base.

Cato has analyzed transactions worth billions of dollars across multiple countries. His contributions include conducting loan portfolio analyses and monitoring macroeconomic trends to guide clients effectively. Contact him at acato@cokergroup.com.

Preface

THE ONGOING GROWTH of the healthcare industry provides ample reasons to write *The Physician Leader's Guide to Affiliation Options: Economics, Tactics, and Real-World Implementation.* This book, therefore, focuses on the topic of affiliations with supplemental advice reflecting strategies and tactics that have emerged over time.

Healthcare providers, sponsors, patients, and third-party payers have discovered many keystone opportunities. Further, consolidation activity continues within the industry, with interest in the private sector, particularly private equity (PE)-backed firms. These influences provide an opportunity to present some relevant discussions and serve as a reference as we discuss new opportunities, scenarios, and situations.

Today's affiliation structures are becoming more evident compared to yesterday's. Specifically, PE firms have gained traction in healthcare through affiliation, integration, and alignment options, which is the main focus of the book. PE firms are real and maintain their market presence. In other words, PE-sponsored deals are continuing and perhaps even expanding in certain specialties, which we explore to update readers on available opportunities.

Hospitals and physician groups continue to form alignments. While employment remains the most prominent form of affiliation, professional services agreements (PSAs) continue to offer an excellent alternative. They are more readily accepted than ever before, and as such, we address PSAs at length.

With these key points in mind, what are our objectives and goals in expounding on the ways physicians are affiliating? Which applications are the best options for implementation for your practice?

The general answer is "we are reviewing everything." Additionally, we explore *new* issues and facets of physician affiliation options. These options are not necessarily new in the sense of a structure that has never been previously applied, but different in the sense of how they affect the overall relationships going forward, from provider to payer to sponsor, owner, and more. We expand upon areas of interest, both new and old. We consider more detailed components of affiliation and provide updated examples.

The chapter descriptions follow.

Chapter 1 — Years and Counting of Affiliation Options. In this chapter, we briefly articulate various structures, models, and related descriptors of affiliation options for physicians. Then, we introduce the newer variations of affiliation between physicians and other parties.

Chapter 2 — Economic Drivers Today. While the economic drivers of earlier years remain, there are new approaches to consider.

Chapter 3 — Current Reasons for Affiliation. The reasons for affiliation remain unchanged, but some sectors have modified the original reasons for affiliation.

Chapter 4 — Review of the Models. Much of this chapter is a historical review of what has and has not worked within the broad definition of affiliation structures. Here, however, we focus more on specific models (such as professional services agreements) that have proven successful over time.

Chapter 5 — Health Systems' Attitudes. While considering hospitals and health systems and their perspectives on physician affiliation, much has changed over recent years that warrant further exploration, discussion, and illustration.

Chapter 6 — Professional Services Agreements versus Employment. This tested option continues. While much of this chapter will entail review and compilation, we will explore the nuances between PSAs and employment today.

Chapter 7 — Private Equity Transactions. Is private equity (PE) alive and well within physician affiliation models, or is it a trend or a fad that will soon expire? We will consider PE in detail, with a look at specific specialties and current PE transaction structures.

Chapter 8 — Merging Practices. Do mergers work? Can they be done in today's environment? Are they affordable? Do they prove worthwhile, both economically, operationally, and relationally? The discussion will consider these points.

Chapter 9 — Clinical Integration Update. Have clinical integration and related agreements morphed into something entirely different? Do they vary by specialty? What are the current trends? This chapter offers up-to-date information.

Chapter 10 — Payer Affiliation Perspectives. Are payers increasingly crossing over to providers? Do they have a prominent role (and will they in the future) in affiliation models with physicians? We will explore these questions.

Chapter 11 — Role of Advisers. Whether advisers are investment bankers, consultants, attorneys, or (most likely) a combination, how has the role of these advisers evolved relative to assisting physicians in affiliation transactions? This chapter looks at what the "quality of earnings process" currently entails.

Chapter 12 — U.S. Healthcare Industry Status. This chapter provides an industry update with regard to physician affiliation models.

Chapter 13 — Legal and Regulatory Update. Compliance and legal parameters are of utmost importance and consideration, calling for this summary of up-to-the-minute topics.

Chapter 14 — Transactions Update: Process, Order, and Other Matters. Some transactions have changed the way the process previously worked. This chapter provides a brief analysis of the typical process for completing these transactions.

Chapter 15 — Federal and State Governments and Healthcare. The government continues to play a huge role in the delivery of healthcare services, in addition to the insurance and reimbursement components. Rather than spending extensive time on what has not changed, we look at some recent changes relative to governmental influence and other issues.

Chapter 16 — The Future: "Clear as Mud." We offer some suggestions and recommendations on how best to strategize the affiliation processes and options for physicians. Although we do not have a "crystal ball," we submit our conclusions and forecasts for the future based on our nearly 40 years of experience working with physicians.

We are now several years post-COVID and hope such a traumatic experience never repeats itself. That could be a game-changer in relation to many of the subjects addressed in this book. We believe the opportunities will continue for all participants within our great U.S. healthcare delivery system.

Our primary purpose is to continue to lay a strong foundation for making sound decisions about the many available affiliation options for physicians. We trust that the readers will find value in this book, and we look forward to hearing about their experiences relating to affiliation options for physicians.

CHAPTER 1.

Years and Counting of Affiliation Options

IN THE PREFACE, WE DISCUSSED the reasons for considering affiliation options among physicians, hospitals, private equity (PE), and other collaboratives. Meanwhile, the U.S. healthcare industry continues to expand, consuming $4.9 trillion (about $15,000 per person in the United States) and 17.6% of the gross domestic product, according to 2023 data from the American Medical Association.[1] The driver is the population that continues to grow older, live longer, and consume more healthcare.

Physicians remain at the core of our healthcare delivery system. They are the ones who make it work or not. Other caregivers are heavily involved — and essential — but it is physicians who drive the delivery. Along with physicians, major health systems, academic and otherwise, from small community hospitals to major tertiary centers, continue to grow and comprise our delivery system.

Considering their vital role, physicians struggle with carrying their heavy load of compliance with multitudes of regulations and the copious demands of medical practice. Though private practice is still a preference, affiliations seem to be a reasonable option. Therefore, we appropriately ask what choices are available to physicians as they look to partner with others.

The answers to the options available in recent years versus those in years past remain the same, although some matters have evolved and matured. As a result, the transactions are more varied and complex. COVID-19 accelerated the shift of physicians away from independent practice toward employment by hospitals, health systems, and corporate entities. Financial instability caused by reduced patient volume and high overhead forced many to seek the security of larger organizations, with nearly 60% of physicians expecting a reduction in independent practices locally.

Since the COVID-19 pandemic, which the World Health Organization (WHO) officially declared began in March 2020, until May 2023, when the WHO declared an end to the public health emergency of international concern, virtually everything seems different.[2] Regardless of the impetus, there is little debate that affiliation transactions are varied and prominent and will continue for many years.

So, what options are available to physicians? As stated, *private practice* is still feasible and often preferable. Nevertheless, most younger physicians completing residency training have substantial debt and knowledge of the "landmines" of private practice. Thus, they run (not even a slow walk) away from owning and operating a private, standalone practice. Even joining private practice with others to help hedge the risks continues to lag in popularity among younger physicians recently out of training.

Academic institutions appeal to many physicians as they provide opportunities for teaching, research, and practicing each specialty's crafts.

Hospital affiliation (as well as health system and partnering affiliations) is still quite popular and, in many cases, a fallback for those who have experienced private practice and are ready to structure something else. Physicians who do not want their own private practice and never have, which is to be expected, often go directly into health system employment.

We have noted a gradual, yet continual, interest in varying models of affiliation with health systems and hospitals. There was a time not that long ago when most affiliations were by *employment*. The health system or hospital provided "W-2" employment to the physician and other providers, including advanced practice providers (APPs). However, over the past decade, *professional services agreements* (PSAs) have become more acceptable and preferable.

PSAs entail a contractual relationship between the physician as the "1099" employee and the health system hospital. A medical directorship, for example, includes a PSA. Co-management agreements encompass contractual agreements via PSAs. However, most of our discussion in this book as we refer to PSAs is what is sometimes called "*employment lite*." Although it is a 1099 relationship, PSAs include everything in services plus compensation structures that W-2 employment entails.

So, the PSAs that we consider have many components of W-2 employment, yet they allow the physicians both independence and autonomy, as the physicians still own and operate a private practice. These PSAs include "wrap-around" structures that are independent PSAs, such as medical directorships, pay-for-call, service line management, clinical co-management, and other services.

Another prominent distinction we encounter today is the trend that will continue (at least through the end of this decade), of the employment-lite PSA. We will devote more discussion to these PSAs, their structure, terms, and conditions throughout this book.

Another major area of evolution in physician affiliation models and structures is the prominence of *private equity investors*. PE means, just as it implies, a consortium of private investors acquiring a healthcare entity such as a medical practice and forming a platform of like businesses, including ancillary services, that grow in value due to the critical mass being assembled. *PE sponsors*, as they are called, provide the infrastructure of management and operations, taking the place of, for example, hospitals that employ or contract with those same physicians.

PE makes no bones about being motivated by profit. Its investors expect a good return on their money. Truly, there is strength in numbers as we have learned over the years, and PE is no exception. Aggregating multiple practices, whether single or multispecialty, provides that critical mass for the benefit of the investor purchasers and the physician sellers in this example, with the promise of a good economic return while mitigating risk.

The capital that many private practicing physicians lack or do not want to risk investing is readily available from the private equity dynamic and the capital that investors provide. All that is required is the PE firm sponsor's partnership, which means the PE firm has majority ownership in leadership and governance control, including determining when and if to recapitalize through a second sale, which is often referred to as the "second bite of the apple" — a concept we will visit later in the book.

Other forms of affiliation include growth in private practice through aggregation of resources and service offerings. This expansion could result from a practice merger where several previously independent private groups consolidate to form a single provider. The benefits are economies of scale on overhead, strength in numbers in payer contracting matters and negotiation positions with hospitals and health systems, and other measures that justify the merger. Quality improvement could even be achieved through a merger, given the pooling of resources, the buying of equipment, and the like, made possible by the critical mass-purchasing power of the larger group.

Although there are spinoffs of the primary affiliation models mentioned, for now, we will maintain a high-level perspective in laying the foundation for more detailed discussion, review, and presentation in the subsequent chapters.

Throughout the years, physicians, hospitals, and other healthcare providers, including the payers themselves, have sought a significant role in the healthcare delivery system and its economic components. Payers are savvy businesspeople and have stepped into all aspects of the delivery system, not just the reimbursement itself, which is still their primary competency and their major goals and objectives for profitability.

Who would have thought 20 years ago that regular (profit or not-for-profit) insurance companies would employ thousands of physicians and APPs? But now they do. Kaiser Permanente and others like it have existed for decades. Yet, they still make up a small percentage of the total number of affiliation structures. Their staff model, as it is sometimes called, will continue to exist. But then there are payers or subsidiaries of payers such as United Healthcare and its Optum division, that have assumed the role of full-fledged providers dealing with the payers, not unlike private practicing physicians.

So, where do we go from here? We will review and update these models in the context of affiliation growth and enhancement and explore new ways, structures, and opportunities.

NUANCES TO THE OPTIONS

As we delve into greater detail relative to the components of deal-making affiliation models, especially between physicians and health systems and/or for-profit companies, we should examine the distinctions that have emerged and are part of the "landscape" of affiliation transactions. In the context of our global discussion, there are several important implications and nuances of the deals between these parties.

Public/Large Company Interests

Corporate America has long had an interest in healthcare, specifically medical practices and their ancillary services, and its interest has increased during the past five years. This has spun off new structures to accommodate their ownership. Examples abound, such as Optum RX, Optum's division of United Healthcare. Companies like Cardinal Health and their parent, Navista™, have acquired what were previously PE-backed companies and have progressed with growth initiatives that include medical practices of various specialties and complementary ancillary services for those practices. Thus, these companies have enjoyed that portion of the healthcare delivery system, which exceeds their traditional services and focus.

Most of these companies are for-profit; thus, they must keep the public marketplace informed of their performance and other matters. Often, these companies have great interest in the core business and services they originally provided, even more than the medical practices and others that they have acquired, complementary to those original services. It is difficult to assess exactly where these companies will take their acquisitions. For example, will they emulate PE and, after a certain period, form the platform, recapitalize, and divest? Possibly (even probably) this will occur, but there is no assurance when we consider their sizeable and often publicly held company structures.

So, while public companies and/or large for-profit entities not necessarily analogous to PE are in the market, doing affiliation deals consistent with our discussion, the emphasis still seems to focus more on hospital/health systems or PE.

Health System Trends

One matter that prompted this book is the myriad details that health systems have introduced and/or expanded within their affiliation transactions, especially with physicians and other providers. In laying a foundation for exploration in later chapters, we will consider these specifics:

Compensation Requirements. Whether PSA or employment or somewhere in between, hospitals are now savvier on their compensation requirements for their employed and/or contracted providers. Like PE arrangements, hospitals are shifting more risk to physicians. Physicians must produce, whether in work RVUs, actual dollars, or both, to be assured a certain amount of compensation. Guaranteed compensation rarely exists and is dwindling. Hospitals are much savvier than before and have more realistic expectations of these providers' production.

Many contractual agreements (e.g., PSA, employment lite, and employment) are being amended to require increased production and/or attaining other performance metrics to achieve comparable levels of pay. For hospitals and health systems, total cash compensation (TCC) is among the top requirements currently — a change from 5–10 years ago.

More Economics at Risk. Relative to compensation, physicians are expected to meet certain economic requirements in contractual or employment arrangements. These areas include quality and other performance metrics tied to hourly-paid functions and related matters. Gone are the days of large guarantees or even "easy-to-attain" performance measures such as co-management/quality/medical directorship duties. More at-risk incentives is a trend that is expected to continue and will be a focal point of many of the deal transactions we discuss in this book.

Quality-Based Pay. As indicated earlier, physicians' compensation will be tied to meeting highly proficient performance measures. If not attained, the provider's compensation is adjusted accordingly. Meeting quality metrics is a part of the affiliation transaction, along with post-transaction compensation.

Flexible Structures. There was a time when hospitals and health systems were universally rigid in their affiliation structures. It was easier and more tenable for the parties to simply opt for employment. Employment continues to be the most popular form of affiliation structure between hospitals and health systems and physicians, but it is not the *only* form and has decreased over recent years.

PSAs are sometimes lesser forms of "full" affiliation or alignment. The employment-lite PSAs continue to be extremely popular, and hospitals and health systems have learned that offering these levels of flexibility allows them to meet competitive challenges while maintaining affiliation opportunities.

Partial Affiliation. While employment is a form of full integration, as are employment-lite PSAs, various individual types of affiliation equate to partial alignment. At one time, the options were essentially employment or nothing, but the choices have changed dramatically. It is now employment, PSA, and even partial components of these models, along with specific carve-outs that allow for separate agreements.

Predominance of Group Think and Group Structure, Including Governance. While many employed physicians are individually contracted through employment directly by the health system, the group-think concept — the practice of approaching problems or issues as matters that are best dealt with by consensus of the group rather than by individuals acting independently — continues to grow. Regarding governance, leadership, authority, and overall strategy, the practice still functions in many ways as a group, without separation among the physician partners and other providers.

Shorter and/or Longer Deals. The duration of transactions with health systems and physician groups varies. In some cases, the effort to build a relationship results in a shorter-term commitment to ensure the relationship will last, with the understanding that the relationship may be extended. On the other hand, longer-term deals are possible from the beginning, especially when the relationship between the health system and the physicians has existed for some time in some other form.

Easy Out for Both Parties. More recent deals allow for an easy unwind with few constraints, although this can vary. Notwithstanding, this form of restrictive covenant preferred by the health system almost always allows the practice to return to private practice.

Noncompete Agreements. While some courts have recently ruled that restrictive covenant noncompetes are less enforceable, this legislation varies by state. In many instances, health systems require restrictive covenants and assume it is enforceable until proven otherwise. Time will tell whether noncompetes continue, but for now, they seem viable.

Antitrust. The Biden administration was bullish on antitrust compliance, even to the point of prioritizing enforceability. The new Trump administration is less aggressive in this role, allowing more variations and thus easier-to-complete transactions. Again, the courts will continue to rule on antitrust issues, and changes could occur in either direction in the next few years.

Ancillaries. Health systems have been more receptive to allowing the practices, particularly under PSA agreements, to continue providing the ancillary services they delivered prior to the affiliation transaction. While hospitals and health systems do not prefer such arrangements, the trend is to allow at least some continued services (see joint ventures discussion, below).

Joint Ventures and Equity Sharing. Joint ventures are comparable to allowing ancillaries to continue after the transaction. These affiliations run the gamut of services from surgery centers to imaging centers and other initiatives. The prominence of joint ventures has increased significantly, which we will discuss extensively in this book.

Referral Sources. While referral sources are burdened with compliance requirements, there are opportunities for physicians to receive and give referrals. Health systems understand this process and, although compensation tied to referrals is prohibited, the practice of building referral bases without remuneration continues to grow.

PE Nuances

Over the past several years, the availability of capital has grown, and PE transactions have become more prominent, yet they differ slightly from the earlier models and, like earlier models, have their pros and cons, which we will review. Hospitals and health systems are not enamored with PE; nevertheless, some structures allow a level of co-existence, as we will discuss.

Some of the refinements that have developed over recent years with PE transactions are considered below.

Limited Funding. While PE has plenty of capital to invest, its management and investors are careful and extremely diligent in committing to funding for the acquisition of practice assets, etc. Whether this is done through a management services organization (MSO) or directly with the practice, depending on state and federal legal constraints, does not matter. The amount of funds invested will have conditions placed on them, as we discuss below and in detail in subsequent chapters.

Earnouts. Earnouts have become more popular with PE transactions and physicians. They entail withholding a certain amount of enterprise value, deferred payment, and are paid based on future performance. Earnouts limit the amount of funds at risk for the PE firm, even though a significant amount is paid at closing. The income scrape and income repair initiatives discussed below are also a part of this equation.

Rollover Equity Spread Out Over Many Individuals and Years. Rollover equity can be the "icing on the cake" for PE transactions. Though not realized for several years (usually at least five to seven) after the initial transaction, this "second bite of the apple" can result in significant return on investment for those equity holders who reinvest part of their enterprise value in the rollover equity. The platform established and anticipated to be growing through acquisition builds greater total value, which equates to a larger rollover equity payout when that recapitalization occurs. While this has always been the case, PE deals recently tilted slightly more total enterprise value to rollover equity.

Physician Mobility Restrictions. Physician mobility restrictions are a part of most PE transactions. The PE firm and/or sponsor must have the assurance that the generators of revenue (primarily the physicians, although APPs as well) will remain not only in full-time (or mostly full-time) practice post-transaction, but will realize comparable (if not greater) levels of productivity. Thus, the physicians' ability to be mobile is limited.

Notwithstanding restrictive covenants, which are also a part of the typical PE transaction (to the extent allowable by regulation and by state), it is imperative to insist that the physicians remain within the enterprise that has been valued and essentially provides the foundation for the entire platform acquired by the PE firm.

Greater Income Scrapes. The income scrape creates value in that it is shifted from income distributed in compensation to the owners of the practice and others. It becomes a greater amount of EBITDA upon which the value is based. (EBITDA is earnings before interest, taxes, depreciation, and amortization.) Notwithstanding the fact that earnouts are more prominent and of a higher amount, and possibly even rollover equity, thus lessening the amount of payout at closing, the income scrape is a major part of the PE transaction. It is growing with recent deals.

Income Repair. Income repair entails opportunities for the post-transaction PE management firm to realize improved return on investment via expense savings and/or revenue enhancements. Revenue enhancements could include improved payer contracting rates, while overhead could be reduced through economies of scale and some consolidation of resources. Thus, income repair is real but often overrated. Therefore, entering a PE transaction requires caution and conservatism in this regard, perhaps unlike it was five years ago.

Recapitalization Requiring More Time. The market will usually dictate whether a PE sponsor capitalizes anew. Such recapitalization may end the relationship in that a new PE partner is now the owner due to purchasing the assets of the practice in the recapitalization process. Many PE-sponsored deals still have recapitalization in their future. Some are being postponed, pending additions to the platform that responds to better market conditions such as lower interest rates, etc. Time will tell whether the recapitalization process is as lucrative as is presented in the PE transaction sales process.

High Cost of Capital. Interest rates play a role in affecting cash flow, working capital, and return on investment. The cost of capital will always be a major factor in the PE process. Conversely, this is not an issue with health systems (at least not directly).

EBITDA Shrinkage. As expenses increase, reimbursement decreases, and other stresses result. Even with critical mass and building of the platform, the ability to generate EBITDA at historically comparable levels is becoming more challenging. PE transactions are largely based upon the ability to create a solid and predictable, even growing, EBITDA. As this becomes more difficult, look for more earnout requirements, holdbacks of certain funds, and even greater income scrapes.

PEs Assuming Less Risk. Over recent years, PE continues to assume a fair amount of risk, but this appears to be lessening as the transactions continue. This is obviously due to the market conditions addressed above (i.e., cost of capital, income scrapes, recapitalization merits, building a platform quickly). These factors continue to need careful monitoring.

Greater Expectations Going into the Transaction. While subjective and opinionated, the recent PE transactions (as opposed to those done five or more years ago) are resulting in greater expectations of a return on investment, higher EBITDA, etc. So, the expectations of everyone, including the buyer, PE sponsor, and the seller (generally a physician practice), are increasing. This will need to be considered in the overall equation, even the fundamental question of whether a practice should pursue and enter affiliation with PE.

SUMMARY

This chapter provided an overview of the various characteristics of physician affiliation that are prominent in today's U.S. healthcare industry. The objective is to lay a foundation for more detailed discussion in later chapters. We will drill down on these points throughout the book.

REFERENCES

1. American Medical Association. Trends in health care spending. American Medical Association. Accessed June 23, 2025. https://www.ama-assn.org/about/ama-research/trends-health-care-spending.
2. World Health Organization. Coronavirus Disease (COVID-19) Pandemic. Accessed May 1, 2026. https://www.who.int/europe/emergencies/situations/covid-19.

CHAPTER 2.

Economic Drivers Today

THE ECONOMIC DRIVERS THAT CURRENTLY INFLUENCE the key players in affiliation structures include:

1. Hospitals and health systems.
2. Physicians and other providers, including advanced practice providers (APPs).
3. Private equity (PE)-backed firms.

As we consider these economic drivers, which are the foundation, we also review the strategies that support the transactions and the financial influencers.

HOSPITALS AND HEALTH SYSTEMS

Hospitals and health systems have wrestled with their strategies for collaborating with physicians and providers — specifically, members of their medical staff — for many years. Initially, both parties were satisfied with at-arm's-length relations, including some limited forms of affiliation, with separation between the private medical practices and the hospital.

Over the past three to four decades, the paradigm has changed significantly. At the start of the transition, hospitals employed physicians, and APPs were under a "W-2" arrangement structure. Hospitals and physicians were disappointed with the outcome of this model and frustrated with the relationship.

Hospitals often paid a significant price to employ physicians, purchasing their practices for far more than they were worth, and then paying them excessive compensation. Further, hospitals lacked the management and administrative infrastructure to properly operate medical practices. Ironically, the economics were quite good for physicians and APPs, while hospitals sustained operational losses. In many cases, financial benefits for the employed staff were too good to be true.

By the turn of the century, the economic losses that hospitals were incurring from employing providers had mounted to prohibitive levels, primarily due to the poor structuring of the transaction which, in many instances, allowed the economics to go unbridled with inadequate incentives to stimulate better performance. As a result, many employed physicians were disengaged and terminated from their employment agreement after a brief duration.

Therefore, hospitals and larger entity health systems, whether for-profit or not-for-profit, went through a dismal period during which they had to revisit, rethink, and in many cases, reassemble their physician enterprise. The economic drivers were not aligned and were far too lucrative, even if they were within compliance boundaries.[1]

As we embarked on the 21st century, hospitals were not only asking themselves why they had chosen to employ so many physicians and APPs, but they were also taking the opportunity, when the contracts allowed, to adjust significantly or terminate altogether. Many physicians returned to private practice, leaving a poor taste for hospital affiliation, but remained active members of a hospital's medical staff. They were seeking other ways to affiliate with their hospitals, involving lesser alignment or integration.

Today, the economic drivers for hospitals and health systems pertaining to their affiliation relationships with physicians and APPs have improved tremendously. Yes, hospitals had to come to a reconciliation with their physician and APP medical staff regarding a realistic economic package, whether by employment, a PSA, or another form of affiliation. As we discuss this further below, from the physician provider perspective, we will consider their point of view strategies (plus how they have dealt with this situation in recent years).

KEY ECONOMIC DRIVERS

What are the keys for hospitals, the current economic drivers, of their affiliation models? Following is a summary of the key points.[2]

1. ***Base Compensation Is Less Guaranteed.*** Once guaranteed pay comprised a sizable portion of the employed and/or otherwise aligned physician/APP compensation. Now, guaranteed income, while still notable, is lower. As a percentage of total cash compensation (TCC), it is often less than two-thirds or as little as one-half.
2. ***Productivity Incentives Are the Norm.*** Originally, most TCC was guaranteed; today, a key economic driver is productivity incentives.

Even under a "fee-for-value" structure, "fee-for-volume" is the norm for both reimbursement and compensation.

3. ***Relative Value Units Have a Huge Place in the Economic Drivers.*** Relative value units, and more specifically, work-only relative value units (wRVUs) are usually the metric that measures units of production. Being "payer blind," they serve as a respectable basis for measuring and compensating provider productivity.
4. ***Quality Pools Usually Exist.*** In a "fee-for-value" paradigm of reimbursement, quality incentives have increased in prominence. However, they continue to be a small portion of TCC.
5. ***Clinical Integration Agreements (CIAs) Have Been Widely Introduced into These Models.*** CIAs can encompass many forms of services that physicians provide to hospitals. Moreover, they are key economic drivers for both quality and efficiency.
6. ***Clinical Co-Management Agreements (CCMAS) Are Often Included but Lack Longevity.*** CCMAs have been a part of CIAs, and usually one or the other is implemented, but not both. CCMAs, while beneficial to both hospitals and physicians, have been only mildly effective. Still, they represent a key economic driver.
7. ***Service Line Management (SLM) Has Been Applied as a Key Economic Driver.*** Hospitals have hesitated to allow "too much" involvement among the physicians. Still, dyad management models have been relatively successful.
8. ***Professional Services Agreements (PSAs) Have Become a Prominent Form of Full Alignment and Entail Key Economic Drivers.*** PSAs that entail the concept of employment lite have been incredibly popular, though to a much lesser degree among hospitals. (See Chapter 6 for a detailed discussion.)
9. ***Hospitals Have Dissected Their PSA Contracts and/or Employment Agreements (EAs) and Their Economic Terms More Than Ever Before.*** Careful analysis and documentation within these legal agreements are essential and have rendered a much better foundation for the success of these structures and overall relationships.
10. ***Restrictive Covenants Have Been an Indirect Key Economic Driver for Hospitals, But Not Surprisingly, Are Unpopular with Physicians.*** While most PSA contracts and EAs entail a restrictive covenant, their

enforceability continues, including those drivers that have at least indirect economic ramifications. The trend, however, is for noncompetes to be less prominent, less legally enforceable, and altogether withdrawn.

11. ***On-Call Compensation Is Now the Norm.*** For many years, one of the most onerous duties of physicians was serving the hospital on call in duties in the emergency department and attending to other patients. The economics of this obligation have changed dramatically. On-call compensation is now the norm, not the exception. This is addressed by specialty and often includes daily stipends at fair market value (FMV), which are deemed reasonable since many of the patients seen by the on-call physician have limited, if any, means of payment. The economic drivers have caused hospitals to recognize the need to compensate physicians for such work.
12. ***Administrative Management Services Are Performed by Physicians for Commensurate Time and Compensation.*** Hospitals have recognized the need to compensate physicians for their administrative management services. Typically, this activity is billed on a per-hour basis, with appropriate documentation of time worked.
13. ***Physicians Are Leaders within Medical Staff Structures.*** Often, employed or otherwise fully aligned physicians are leaders within the medical staff structure. While not a key economic driver for integration, depending on the services and their depth, physicians may be compensated for their time.

Hospitals and health systems have improved their management structures for physician enterprise operations and have considered the economic drivers of affiliation. This thought process has resulted in remarkable improvements in both the relationships and the overall fiscal performance of that physician enterprise. Still, there are areas to improve. Nonetheless, these economic drivers have undergone significant adjustments from their original establishment. Overall, this improvement is good for the industry.

ECONOMIC DRIVERS FOR PHYSICIANS AND OTHER PROVIDERS

While the list of economic drivers described most, if not all, of the economic drivers, we approached that discussion from the perspective of hospitals and health systems' view. Now we address the economic drivers from the physicians' and other providers' points of view.

1. ***Direct Operational Results.*** Physicians primarily focus on the "bottom line," especially in private groups. As a partner in that group, their compensation is based on the bottom line. In a hospital or even a PE organization (see below for that discussion) an affiliation structure, along with direct operating results, of the overall income, often measured in the form of earnings before income taxes depreciation and amortization (EBITDA), is equally important and in focus.

   There are nuances to bottom-line calculations. First to consider is whether a cash basis or accrual basis of accounting is applied. The cash basis is usually used for smaller groups and for their own internal tabulation and record-keeping. The accrual basis is the more accurate methodology for correctly stating financial statement performance, including the income statement and balance sheet. Nonetheless, either methodology carries vital information relative to the overall economic drivers of the practice. EBITDA is a prominent and consistent measure of operating results. Typically, this excludes non-cash items, and it also does not consider the effect of income taxes. Therefore, this measure directly assesses the overall performance within the practice and does not consider the effect of depreciation and amortization, both of which are non-cash expenses. Depreciation and amortization, as well as income taxes, which are a definite cost attributable to for-profit entities but are not usually considered for the measurement of overall performance and on a comparative basis.

   Direct operating results influence many decisions within the practice and are a measurement of fiscal viability. It also forms the basis for the determination of value, especially for purposes of acquisition/sale to a hospital or health system and to PE.

   For years, direct operating results have varied as to their measurement for accounting reporting purposes. More recently, the methodologies for presenting direct operating results have become consistently applied and, thereby, comprising a more authentic and usable metric.

2. ***Professional Fees.*** The amount of professional fees generated impact the overall economic drivers of any medical practice. Professional fees

are those charged to the patient for services performed by physicians and APPs. Whether in a hospital or clinic or some other provider facility, professional fees, coupled with technical or facility fees, make up the overall revenue derived from such services.

For physicians, professional fees are associated with their work (along with APPs) and are often measured in *gross charges*. Gross charges are unadjusted for contractual allowances and other discounts. At some point, gross charges are then converted to *net charges,* which are after the adjustments, discounts, and contractual allowances.

In both cases, charges do not represent the actual dollars received. *Net collections* represent that amount and should be close to net charges, even though there may be some additional discounts for bad debts and other deductions. Even on an accrual basis of accounting, the net charged total should be adjusted to reflect write-offs or other reductions to that total, ultimately representing the actual dollars collected.

No matter the accounting methodology, professional fees are representative of the physician's and APP's work product and the reimbursement and payer mix structure of the organization with whom they are affiliated. Obviously, the volume of charges and collections can vary, depending on the payer mix, payer contracting rates, and other related structures. Therefore, the economic drivers are often leveled on the playing field of measurement through some standardized unit of production measurement.

Typically, that unit of production measurement is relative value units. Relative value units comprise three components: the operational component, malpractice, and the professional component, also referred to as the *work* component. wRVUs, therefore, are the measurement that provides consistency across the board in terms of productivity. wRVUs, for example, are payer blind, and therefore make no difference as to the ability of the patient to pay and the third-party payer that supports the same.

RVUs therefore are the most prominent measurement of productivity, and in many instances, are the key metric that determines compensation over and above a certain guaranteed pay amount.

3. ***Ancillary Services Fees.*** Ancillaries are services that are performed separately from the professional fees and are not part of the revenue component. Typically, the revenue components are technical or facility-based fees the physician or any other healthcare provider, such as a hospital or health system, realizes from the provision of the services by the physician or APP. The charge for the facility is separate from the professional charge. However, some payer contracts include a combination of professional and technical services, referred to as a *global fee*.

   Although the global fee may be the methodology for billing, it is possible to separate, from an accounting perspective, the professional (vis-à-vis through wRVUs) from the technical dollars billed. It is also possible to separate the technical fees with both measures being key economic drivers of the affiliation model.

   Simply said, it is rare that any facility or technical fees are generated without the support, direction, and oversight of the physician/APP. Therefore, technical fees from ancillary services such as imaging and other diagnostic testing are inclusive of the economic drivers within affiliation models, as they are structured today.
4. ***Units of Production.*** We discussed this by introducing the concept of relative value units. Units of production could be measured in other areas, such as the time spent with the patient or performing the procedure, and considering metrics that might be more accurate for measuring productivity. Without question, the most prominent measurement of units of production are RVUs.
5. ***Revenue Derived from Contractual Agreements.*** In addition to professional and technical fees derived from clinical services performed, physicians and APPs may generate revenue via a professional services agreement (PSA). Such agreements entail work completed by the physician for specific services. Examples include on-call for emergency department patients, medical directorships providing the clinical supervision over a particular service within the hospital or other healthcare provider, clinical co-management agreements (CCMAs) wherein physicians are asked to collectively manage with the hospital areas within a particular specialty or service line, and clinical integration agreements such that myriad services entail the

parties being clinically integrated through common systems and related technology. These may encompass a significant workload for physicians, depending on the specialty and, without question, require the clinical training and expertise of physicians and sometimes, on a more limited basis, APPs.

6. ***Support of Resident Training and Other Related Services.*** Again, these are typically subject to a PSA, but entail specific stipends paid to physicians for oversight and management of residents and other healthcare providers — usually not full-time practicing physicians at that point.

Overall, these economic drivers make up the key components for physicians and APPs. Without the physicians' expertise and the ability to bill and receive reimbursement from the payers for such services, the entire healthcare system would not function.

PE-BACKED ECONOMIC DRIVERS

Fundamentally, PE firms, or those backed by PE, are 100% for-profit entities and are interested in generating a significant return on investment. The significance of these opportunities can vary depending on the situation, but unlike other healthcare providers, PE-backed firms are primarily motivated by the opportunities that healthcare entity investments entail. As a result, most are not interested in marginal profit/EBITDA status, as historically unprofitable healthcare providers have been in the past. They may be willing to invest in entities that show potential, but they are usually only interested in profitable organizations.

Their structure will vary, and we will not explain more details other than to recognize certain terms that are characteristically economic drivers for PE affiliation transactions. We consider the key ones, below, presented in the form of a glossary of terms, followed by further explanation.

1. ***Revenue Enhancement.*** Development of specific strategies to grow the collected billings and to increase the billings via improved payer contracting rates, ancillary services with margins, and all other strategies to promote and realize greater revenue per unit of service (i.e., patient, procedure, consultation, etc.).

   Most healthcare entities have alternative forms of revenue generation that are accretive to the core business. Most healthcare providers view their core business, and particularly in the context of PE affiliation, with medical practices, and thus, the professional fees that are realized from their services. Enhancement of revenue can come in the form of additional expertise, generating more professional fees, but usually more so in the form of ancillary services (see #5 below). These give them more flexibility in supplementing, albeit augmenting, the revenue from professional fees.

2. ***Income Repair***. The ability to increase revenue and profitability to offset a decrease in annual income based on the income scrape (see #6 below). The goal is to procure areas of increased revenue as an offset to the income reduction/scrape.

   While PE-backed firms are concerned about profitability, they also seek stability and the continuation of a strong provider base, including physicians and APPs. With the degree of income scrape, PE sponsors are concerned about ways to supplement the income loss from the scrape. Thus, opportunities abound to do so. This could include joint equity transactions for ancillary services, additional stipends for specific services such as on-call work at hospitals, and arrangements like clinical co-management agreements and medical directorships.

3. ***Return on Investment (ROI) and Growth***. The realization of dollars invested against dollars earned, with the latter the numerator and the former the denominator; usually stated on a percentage basis. The growth of such ROI would be realized through specific strategies to expand the revenue base.

   ROI for PE firms is the most critical economic lever they seek to pull. Bottom-line growth and profitability, as measured by EBITDA, are primary goals. It is an ongoing objective of their investment. Without this growth in both revenue and profitability, the venture will be deemed less than successful.

4. ***Rollover Equity and Recapitalization Proceeds.*** Equity holders in the target company reinvest a portion of their ownership stake into a new equity capital structure established by the acquiring firm. Often, this new company, or "Newco," is the platform entity being acquired or one that has already been purchased.

   When a healthcare entity such as a medical practice sells the assets of its healthcare services entities, the expectation of some of those proceeds being reinvested is in the rollover equity. This is manifested in the ultimate decision for that PE sponsor to recapitalize — meaning that the recapitalization entails a sale to another, usually PE-backed entity, for its new investment. The rollover equity's value has increased via the expanded platform of services accretive to each rollover investor. Thus, the second "bite of the apple" is manifested in additional returns for that initial seller.

5. ***Ancillary Services***. Medical and other related services adjunct to medical practice or other healthcare entities, involving something other than professional fees (i.e., technical/global fees/ facility fees, rental income, etc.).

   Ancillary revenues are a major part of the PE economic drivers. Without the ability to expand and grow these services, such as ambulatory surgery centers and imaging centers, which generate technical fees or other forms of revenue, the PE venture will not meet its economic objectives.
6. ***Income Scrape***. A reduction in compensation to allow the practice to generate positive EBITDA on a go-forward basis. The reduction of compensation to the owners of the healthcare entity that is being acquired by PE is what creates the EBITDA of that entity, which is then paid at closing. This income scrape, however, can be costly to individual physicians, especially younger providers within a group who desire more compensation. Thus, income repair (#2 above) is essential.
7. ***Benefits***. These represent specific components of compensation tied to in-kind performance and/or insurance benefits and other mechanisms that augment and/or supplement the compensation package for an employee, whether provider, staff, or any other position. Typically, these are IRS W-2 employees, while contract laborers are 1099 employees, paid extra to cover their costs of benefits.

   Although benefits are important for many reasons, they can also be costly. These include the predictable ones, such as health and life and disability insurance, but also can include retirement/401K plans. However, they can raise costs and lower EBITDA, thus making it a challenge to maintain a competitive benefits package for the PE-affiliated entity.

FIGURE 2.1. Economic Drivers

Description*	Hospitals and Health Systems	Physicians and APP Providers	PE-Backed Firms
Production			
Professional fees	✓	✓	✓
Technical	✓	✓	✓
Ancillaries	✓	✓	✓
Other	✓	✓	✓
Expenses			
Operating	✓		✓
Personnel	✓		✓
Compensation	✓	✓	✓
Research	✓		
Academic	✓		
Consultative	✓	✓	✓
Service Line Performance	✓		
Physician Enterprise	✓		
Limits of Production	✓	✓	✓
Contractual Revenue	✓	✓	✓
Hospital Department	✓		
Acceptable Loss	✓		
Clinical Integration	✓	✓	
Revenue Cycle Management	✓	✓	✓
Rollover Equity Value			✓
Income Repair			✓
Income Scrape			✓
Tangible Assets Value	✓	✓	✓
Intangible Assets Value			✓
Downstream Revenue	✓		

*Economic Drivers – Subject of interest

In summary, PE firms focus on economic levers, perhaps more than any other potentially involved party in affiliation transactions. Figure 2.1 summarizes the key economic drivers for each of the three main affiliation options: hospitals and health systems, physicians and APPs, and PE-backed firms. Interestingly, most of these drivers apply to all three of the potential affiliation entities. Some could apply more than others to a particular situation.

But it is interesting that even within a not-for-profit scenario (more likely a partial not-for-profit scenario), economic drivers are not merely important; they are essential.

SUMMARY

Chapter Two is dedicated to key economic drivers. A couple of interesting observations have resulted. First, it is characteristically interesting that so many of the same economic drivers apply to whomever the affiliation partner is. Hospitals and health systems, physician practices, and PE-backed firms all share in many common economic drivers. Within a not-for-profit setting, the entity still must sustain appropriate cash flow and working capital, along with excess earnings margins, to survive both in the near term and in the long term. PE-backed firms have no apologies for realizing (demanding) adequate ROI within their healthcare affiliation structure. Private groups and physicians share similar needs while also protecting their current compensation totals.

As we continue to analyze aspects of physician affiliation strategies, this chapter is fundamentally essential to ensure that adequate economic drivers are in play and being realized.

REFERENCES

1. We are not providing an opinion on the merits of these original structures of hospitals and health systems employing physicians and other providers. We merely point out that, retrospectively, they were without financial substantiation.
2. The list of Key Economic Drivers, like many resources in this book, represents a generalization of characteristics and keystone discussion points. We readily acknowledge exceptions and variances to these generalizations. However, we represent them as pervasive, characteristic of many, if not most, situations.

CHAPTER 3.

Why Should I Affiliate?

As the 21st century moves into its second quarter of 2026, stress points continue throughout the healthcare industry. These emanate from all perspectives: payer, provider, and consumer alike. In this chapter, we explore the basic reasons for affiliation and discuss the core challenges that currently and prospectively exist for all.

Technology is the industry's linchpin and is widely embraced. The costs are significant and difficult to absorb without affiliation. Despite high costs, technology provides fuel for advancements in both clinical and administrative processes. Twenty years ago, the big push for electronic health records (EHRs) initially met with intense resistance. Today, virtually no one operates under a manual medical record system.

Technology enables payers and providers to communicate electronically. The providers are able to combine historical patient records where clinical integration has occurred, making all aspects of the patient's care and health history available. This results in tremendous improvements in outcomes and overall patient satisfaction.

The healthcare industry has also embraced artificial intelligence (AI). AI applications in healthcare are not just on the horizon; they are present and operational now.

AFFILIATION EMPHASIS

While the models and structures of affiliation are still pertinent, the core emphasis is less on the structure and more on the economics and the quality outcomes of affiliation. Although we can make a case for the consolidation of providers, perhaps even with payers, too, in the sense that clinical performance is much more successful when these parties work together and have a common goal, such as the health and welfare of the populace, affiliation is an obvious choice.

Gone are the days when providers were disjointed, independent, and non-communicative with each other. In recent years, the affiliation structures have been the fuel to drive healthcare for more efficiency, better clinical care, and cost savings. While affiliations present some legal challenges, such as antitrust, Stark, and anti-kickback issues, the ultimate compelling result is cost consolidation. *Affiliation* is the keystone concept today and in the future!

CONSOLIDATION TRENDS IN HEALTHCARE

Consolidation within the healthcare industry has been a consistent trend for at least the past three decades, if not longer. The primary focus of this consolidation is among providers, particularly physician groups and hospital or health system entities. These types of affiliations account for the majority of transactions in the sector. In more recent years, private equity (PE) firms have emerged as prominent players, seeking opportunities in healthcare across a wide range of entities, from medical practices to hospitals and health systems. This involvement by PE has further accelerated the consolidation process.

Multiple driving forces are behind this ongoing consolidation. Economic considerations and the pursuit of clinical quality improvements are at the forefront. As these affiliations continue to grow, the provider segment in the United States likely will become increasingly consolidated. However, this movement does not necessarily signal a single-payer, government-sponsored program nationwide. Instead, consolidation efforts often occur within specific regions, communities, and among for-profit and not-for-profit health systems.

The rationale for consolidation is multifaceted. Often, it is a strategic effort to achieve cost savings and enhance revenue. Additionally, social pressures play a significant role, especially as businesses — both private and public — remain major supporters of healthcare through employee group health plans. These organizations bear a substantial portion of healthcare costs and, as such, influence the push for consolidation through community sentiment and broader societal expectations.

The general consensus among stakeholders is clear: Continued support for the healthcare industry, particularly in the context of employment, will require further consolidation. This will lead to greater efficiencies, cost reductions, and sustained or increased revenue.

EDUCATION OF THE CONSUMER AND THE PROVIDERS

We have learned a lot over recent years about how best to structure provider-affiliated models; the result has been improved cost control and quality of care. Again, technology has been a huge contributor to this efficiency. Technology alone, however, through its cost savings, requires more consolidation of providers and even some payers.

For example, working hand in hand with the government's component of the payer side (i.e., Medicare, Medicaid, TRICARE, etc.) has proven a valuable consortium for driving down costs and controlling reimbursement. Many would argue that this is still an imperfect system, and they are likely correct. Considering all things, affiliation strategies have proven to be a positive contributor to the overall delivery of healthcare services and they will undoubtedly continue. Providers and payers, but especially the public, the consumers of healthcare, must be educated and fully understand how healthcare works best and how we best work together, eliminating greediness by any single party and eliminating unethical and non-compliant behavior. All these improvements cultivate a more efficient healthcare delivery system. Affiliation structures will complement these accomplishments as we consider increasing consolidation.

RURAL PROVIDER CHALLENGES

Rural healthcare providers, including physicians, ancillary services, and hospitals, face challenges that threaten their viability. The COVID-19 pandemic proved that rural healthcare providers could not sustain such a tremendous challenge without affiliation. As a result, new ways to provide care emerged — most notably, telemedicine. Although telemedicine was widely accepted and proved beneficial, especially in rural areas, as the COVID-19 pandemic waned, the emphasis on telemedicine has diminished as a preferred form of care. Clearly, doctors prefer to treat their patients in person.

Many rural hospitals have had no choice but to sell to larger suburban or metropolitan systems to support them. This inevitably limits the services they can provide locally, with more specialized services transferred to the main hospital. Specialized services such as general surgery, orthopedics, and some internal medicine sub-specialties may continue to be available locally, but unhappy patients have had no choice but to obtain other, more specialized care elsewhere or locally on a limited basis.

As a result, rural providers often struggle to adjust their affiliation strategies. Indications are that this situation will likely accelerate. Economic drivers control these decisions, and the providers themselves, primarily physicians, have less desire to travel to rural facilities to provide care. When they do, it is often for consultations; few procedures are performed locally.

In many instances, there must be partnering structures through which the rural providers receive financial and operational assistance in their provision of care. As a result, the affiliation structures among rural providers with their urban/suburban partners have matured and progressed. Gone are the days of merely working together. Legal structures that entail ownership of the rural provider facilities, especially hospitals, are common. When this occurs, the physicians and other providers within the communities are employed directly by the parent organization or indirectly through ownership at the local level. The parent company health system supplies capital and resources to support these practices. Critical access hospitals (CAHs) have become common in rural communities, and while they provide many benefits, they are not sufficient to limit the need for affiliation strategies between rural and suburban/urban hospitals.

If another pandemic occurs (hopefully not), will our country be better prepared, including the providers? It is uncertain. Nonetheless, consolidation was and will continue to be a viable response to pandemic events. These responses will be monitored carefully as we continue to seek ways to provide cost-effective and high-quality healthcare.

DIVERSE CULTURAL NEEDS AND EMPHASIS

Since the country's founding, not-for-profit health systems have thrived. The first medical society was formed in Boston in 1735. Fifteen years later, in 1750, the first general hospital was established in Philadelphia. In 1765, the Medical College of Philadelphia was founded. Two years later, the medical department of King's College was established in New York and, in 1770, awarded the first American MD.[1]

While not-for-profit entities have the advantage of not paying taxes, they still face the same or more challenges concerning compliance and proper structuring of transactions to endure as a long-standing provider affiliation.

Providing care, regardless of the patient's ability to pay, is at the foundation of not-for-profit healthcare entities. As expected, this causes economic challenges, with these institutions having to pass greater costs onto those who are insured, through either government insurance programs or private commercial ones. Not-for-profit healthcare organizations may also struggle to adhere to the government's rules and regulations relating to Stark and anti-kickback, antitrust, and others. This compliance also affects the for-profit entities and the transactional components of affiliation, and the various models previously reviewed.

Some not-for-profits place an even higher level of scrutiny on what they will be willing to do (or not do) within a transactional affiliation structure and setting. For example, while professional services agreements (PSAs) are somewhat popular with not-for-profit institutions, many hospitals are guarded about how far they will go with a particular PSA employment-lite structure. Other not-for-profit bodies will enter a traditional PSA with few enhancements.

Although often reticent to allow a global professional services agreement, these institutions will permit one if the not-for-profit health system is in control of the revenue cycle, including staffing the billing and collections departments for the practices to which they are affiliated. A global PSA in healthcare is a strategic partnership model wherein a hospital or health system contracts with a physician practice to provide professional clinical services, while the practice maintains its independent corporate structure. The hospital takes over the entire revenue cycle (billing, collections, and payer contracting), but, unlike a traditional PSA, the physician practice remains responsible for all its own operating costs, including compensation, benefits, and overhead.

PSAs are therefore still popular, but as the future unfolds, PSAs will probably come under even greater scrutiny, not just for not-for-profits, but for-profits as well. Is this a reason to avoid PSAs? Not at all. But it would be wise to obtain legal and consulting advice to establish a firm PSA strategy.

Faith-based organizations play a foundational role in providing healthcare in the United States, and their beliefs can play a role in affiliation structures. Religious orders follow certain standards. While these criteria may not directly affect the structuring of an affiliation transaction, they almost always affect it indirectly.

For example, there are over 650 Catholic-based hospitals throughout the United States[2] and approximately 22 Jewish hospitals.[3] In addition, there are many evangelical groups with their own unique beliefs about healthcare. The beliefs of all these groups can affect methods of care, such as surgical procedures, blood transfusions, and reproductive health. These factors can affect the affiliation transaction structure.

REASONS TO TRANSCEND TO AFFILIATION AND RELATED TERMS AND CONDITIONS

Although there are exceptions, many providers today have already affiliated or will soon look for ways, both moderate and full, to join others. Thus, searching for diverse partners, even variations of the traditional partnership structures, is apt to continue and may generate more complex and overly complicated affiliation structures that incorporate pieces of the basic structures that currently exist, such as PSAs and employment, and fashion them into new structures. As a result, providers who would have never considered partnerships before will now consider them.

Third-party payer insurance companies, for example, have prominence in their ownership and employment of physician practices. This organizational structure dates back many years, when Kaiser Permanente started this trend in their staff model by employing most of their providers, especially physicians, years before hospitals started employing practices. We expect the continuation of diverse types of partnerships in the near- and longer-term future.

Multiple partners may also be a possibility. For example, it has become common for three partners to be involved: (1) the physician practice, (2) the health system, and (3) another independent investor/operator entity. Partners who previously viewed each other as almost hostile competitors and/or payers are now open to consideration for full partnering. This change in thinking has resulted in more transactions and stranger collaborators than we would have ever thought, even as recently as 10 years ago.

VARYING MODELS OF AFFILIATION

This book does not spend a great deal of time defining and providing details related to the basic affiliation models. Basic models have not changed in the sense that they are the standard bearers for affiliation. We review each of them briefly here:

- *Clinical co-management agreements (CCMAs).* CCMAs have been around for a long time and have been effective to an extent, but usually they are not a standalone-only form of affiliation. They may be a part of a wrap-around relationship, wherein a PSA or employment is the primary, foundational piece of the arrangement. CCMAs will continue to evolve and, in fact, their nomenclature is sometimes different in that many that began as truly co-management have ended up similar to some form of PSA. Call them what you like, they still abound in specific clinical goals and objectives to achieve higher and better quality of care.
- *Various forms of employment.* Employment will vary, even though we are still bound to the "W-2" relationship. This means that benefits are implicit along with their compensation and usually encompass a detailed employment contract. However, some employment among hospitals has changed in that they allow much more freedom and independence. Certain groups are allowed to stand alone at times, separated, and presented to the public as a continuation of the group they had always been.

  Group practice subsidiary (GPS) models exist in which the physicians are treated as independent entities (while still fully employed) and enjoy an elevated level of independence and autonomy. This includes developing their own ancillaries and joint ventures with the health system partner. Thus, the employment model will continue to be the single greatest form of affiliation with various nuances.
- *Professional Services Agreements.* Employment-lite PSAs arrived on the scene in the last 15 or so years. In these arrangements, the physician providers are independent contractors. They keep their practice intact as a separate legal entity that completes the contractual relationship terms and conditions with the health system or PE. We expect this form to continue and grow, though with certain fine-tuning of structures from both compliance and operational preference standpoints. PSAs have proven their value and have stood the test of time and compliance.
- *Hospital service line management.* Often a part of a clinical co-management agreement, service line management has a focus such that

hospitals with great vision and trust allow physician specialists to be actively involved, typically in a dyad model, in management and overall administration. This allows the physicians (who receive compensation for their time and effort in these roles) to provide excellent input and contributions to the overall operations and performance of service lines. These forms of affiliation should continue to grow as hospitals recognize superior results through service line management agreements and thus the value of their physician specialists.

- ***Expanded role of physicians.*** Physicians' roles in organizations have continued to expand in recent years. The value of physicians in administrative and clinical leadership roles is recognized more than ever before. Physicians are an essential part of the healthcare delivery system. Whether their work and recognition of their involvement is contractual or more casual (which we do not recommend), they are here to stay — as they should. The institution of healthcare centers on physicians.
- ***Market value compensation.*** This is the rule of the day for these transaction structures. Stark anti-kickback and other regulations prevent payment to physicians based on the number of referrals and anything other than fair market value (FMV) compensation for any service, no matter the model. Employment, PSA, and any other form of affiliation all require scrutiny of the compensation structure. Typically, a fair market value expert reviews and gives an opinion on the agreement. This person is an independent adviser who understands the complexities of the care and services to be delivered by that provider whose compensation is under consideration. This scrutiny is imperative and will continue to be under the employment agreement.

Thus, while the models of affiliation have remained essentially the same over the years, we emphasize the variation, nuances, and complexities as they have evolved in recent years. We will review these subjects through the remaining chapters of this book.

PRIVATE PRACTICE HOLDOVERS

Private practice continues to exist, though it is becoming less common. Merging with other groups is a more effective way to address the desire to continue in private practice. As supergroups form, giving them more influence with hospitals and health systems, payers, and other competitive providers of like mind and specialty are merging.

Mayo Clinic, Cleveland Clinic, and other large practices continue to flourish and provide excellent care with an elevated level of efficiency. Their ability to coordinate care across a full continuum of specialties is remarkable and outdistances the traditional approach of providers. Attempts to communicate and clinically integrate often fall short, while major clinics like Mayo and Cleveland meet these challenges masterfully.

Nonetheless, with the ingenuity of capitalism, the private sector largely in control of healthcare in the United States, and a willingness to become more efficient while delivering optimal quality of care, the result is positive. And in the private practicing sector, those holdovers will continue to have an active role in these processes, partnering with health systems, insurance companies, and others to ensure efficiency.

Table 3.1 summarizes key variables considered by various parties typically involved in physician and other healthcare provider affiliations. The line-item description represents the entity involved (e.g., physician practice, hospital health system, PE firm, and others).

We believe the table accurately summarizes each entity's keystones. Obviously, these depend on the entity's perspective and whether they are a "buyer" or "seller."

As noted, many of the keystone goals and objectives are characteristic for multiple entities. For example, rural hospitals (the first listed in Figure 3.1) "check the box" on virtually every one of the keystone goals and objectives.

The variable nature of these goals still exists and, thus, the risk of compartmentalizing these goals and objectives exists, specifically with the entity involved. Nonetheless, we believe it is a valuable tool, especially for those less experienced and accustomed to working on such transactions of affiliation.

SUMMARY

The basic rationales for collaboration have become commonplace and overlap, depending upon the parties involved. The approach in this chapter is to consider in depth the clinical, administrative, financial, and operational considerations relative to the reasons for affiliation. Moreover, we have

TABLE 3.1. Summary of Key Variables

Entity by Origin	Affiliation Structures/Goals/Objectives (see legend)
Rural Hospitals	1, 2, 3, 4, 5, 6, 7, 8, 9, 10, 11, 12, 13, 14, 15, 16
Urban Hospitals	1, 2, 3, 4, 5, 6, 7, 8, 9, 10, 11, 12, 13, 14, 15, 16
Diverse Health Systems	1, 2, 3, 4, 5, 6, 7, 8, 9, 10, 11, 12, 13, 14, 15, 16
Academic Hospitals	1, 2, 3, 4, 5, 6, 7
CAH Hospitals	1, 2, 3, 4, 6, 7, 8, 9, 10, 11, 12, 13, 14, 15, 16
PCPs	1, 2, 3, 4, 7, 8, 10, 11, 12, 13, 14, 15, 16
APPs	1, 2, 3, 4, 5, 7, 8, 12, 13, 14, 15, 16
SCPs	1, 2, 3, 4, 5, 6, 7, 8, 9, 10, 11, 12, 13, 14, 15, 16
For-Profit Payers	2, 3, 7, 8, 10, 13, 14, 15
Not-for-Profit Payers	3, 7, 8, 10, 12, 13, 14, 15, 16
Government Payers	3, 7, 8, 10, 12, 13, 14, 15, 16
Private Equity Sponsors	1, 2, 3, 4, 5, 7, 8, 11, 12, 13, 14, 15
Public Equity Investors	1, 2, 3, 4, 5, 7, 8, 11, 12, 13, 14, 15

Legend

1. Compensation enhancements
2. Fiscal viability – profitability
3. Quality
4. Employment
5. PSAs
6. Carve-out PSAs
7. Ability to deliver services
8. Ancillary services growth
9. Telemedicine
10. Co-management roles
11. Clinical Integration
12. Valuation
13. Closing Proceeds
14. Services – clinical
15. Services – administrative
16. Legal, compliance considerations

taken the basic affiliation model, such as employment and PSA, and delved more deeply into the various forms, strategies, and tactics related to these types of affiliation.

REFERENCES

1. Rook D. *The History of Healthcare in America: From the 1700s to Now.* JP Griffin Group. Accessed April 27, 2026. https://cdn2.hubspot.net/hubfs/457237/JP_Griffin_Group_The_History_of_Healthcare_in_America.pdf.
2. U.S. Catholic Health Care. Catholic Health Association of the United States. 2025. https://www.chausa.org/docs/default-source/about/catholic-health-care-in-the-united-states.pdf?sfvrsn=a745daf2_3.
3. Halperin E. The rise and fall of the American Jewish hospital. *Acad Med.* 2012;87(5):p 610–614. https://doi.org/10.1097/acm.0b013e31824d563c.

CHAPTER 4.

Review of Affiliation Models

THIS CHAPTER DELVES DEEPER into the models of affiliation, integration, and alignment typically forged between hospitals and physicians. Figure 4.1 describes the various models, dividing them into three major classifications: limited, moderate, and full.

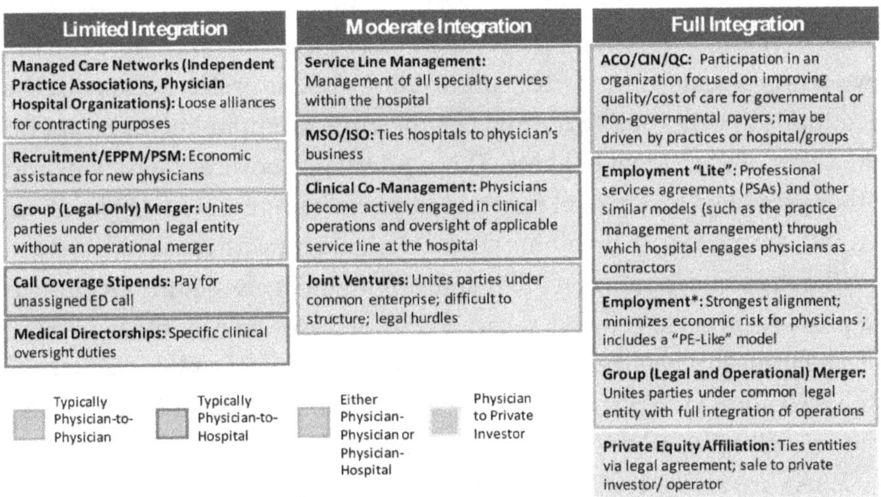

FIGURE 4.1. Levels of Integration Models

Not surprisingly, these models have evolved over recent years and are primarily applicable to the "moderate" and "full" forms of integration.

PSAs are discussed here primarily in the context of integration, alignment, and affiliation, which are synonymous terms. There are standard PSAs that stand alone, representing a physician and a hospital, for example, based on the specific merits of that "job." These would fall into either the basic or moderate forms of integration, referring to Figure 4.1.

EMPHASIS ON PSAs AND EMPLOYMENT — SIMILARITIES AND DIFFERENCES

Some practices are merging to become "super groups" and continue their private structure. To an extent, affiliation with private equity (PE), where PE sponsors develop an expanded platform of similar provider entities, is becoming more prominent. For example, a PE firm may initially acquire a moderate to large orthopedic practice and, within three years, not only have added more orthopedic and/or other musculoskeletal practices but have complemented them with ancillary services.

Five years ago, PSAs were growing in popularity but were limited in quantity. Today, this is hardly the case. PSAs ("employment lite") are not only popular, they are also functional and have proven to be fully legally compliant.

PSAs have gained popularity largely because physicians tend to prefer them over employment once they understand the difference between the two arrangements. A key factor contributing to these preferences is that the economic benefits of a PSA should be the same as employment, except for the value of additional benefits. This equivalency ensures physicians and other providers receive full functionality and compensation, typically as "1099" contractors, maintaining financial alignment with the health system.

The differences between PSAs and employment are significant enough to provide physicians with a sense of comfort, especially at the beginning of a relationship between a hospital/health system and a physician group. The PSA allows the physician practice to remain private and independent, though fully aligned with the health system.

PSAs are also a feasible way to build trust between physicians and hospitals. The process can be likened to the analogy of a child who crawls before learning to walk: The PSA represents the "crawling" phase while employment represents the "walking" phase.

Models of PSAs

The models of PSAs are briefly summarized here:

- **Traditional PSA.** The hospital/health system employs all non-providers and manages the practice, with the providers being independent and outside of employment.
- **Global PSA.** All administrative and professional components within the global PSA are independent, with the reimbursement coming from the hospital/health system employer.
- **Partial/Hybrid Carve-Out PSA.** The practice is contracted for a specific component, service, area of care, or location. A classic example

is a specialty practice in a rural area that the hospital wants to grow and expand, but the private practice is not willing to assume all the risks. Thus, the physicians are protected from some risks (but not all) via the PSA, with the hospital bearing the start-up costs and ongoing administrative expenses through a traditional or global PSA structure.

There are standard PSAs that stand alone, representing a physician and a hospital, for example, based on the specific merits of that "job." These would fall into either the basic or moderate forms of integration, referring to Figure 4.1.

- **Joint Ventures (JVs) and Equity Sharing.** With some distinctions, these relationships are part of the PSA strategy and allow for even more flexibility (albeit subject to specific compliance requirements) to attain the objectives to which both seller and buyer (and in this case, partner) aspire.

  One form of joint venture that has successfully melded physicians and health systems, along with other healthcare services entities, entails the syndication offering to partner in such ventures. Often, the developer of the initiative, such as an ambulatory surgery center, will set aside equity interests for sale to interested investors such as physicians/surgeons. Thus, the syndication is a group of investors that pool resources to undertake a transaction initiative that may not be as easily done alone.

  The syndication allows for an arm's-length investment vehicle that offers ownership for a specific venture. It allows various healthcare providers to invest and, by structure, do so through the syndicate and not directly with the actual fellow healthcare providers. Thus, the syndicate averts the direct challenges and potential conflicts that often occur when a direct equity stake exists. This "protective veil" helps to avoid almost inevitable conflicts in governance and other decisions relative to operations of the initiative.
- **PE-like Models.** Over time, this model has been considered, especially for a large, single-specialty (or even multispecialty) group practice, where many of the characteristics of a PE transaction can be applied with some variables. But overall, this model has not caught on for many reasons. For example, the amount of capital required upfront at closing, which is part of the typical PE deal, is atypical for hospitals and

health systems and medical practices. Nonetheless, PE deals are worth mentioning and potentially considering, although few examples of this model or even variations thereof have, in our experience, resulted, and we doubt they will be in the future.

PSA Evolution

The evolution and maturation of PSAs is remarkable. Over the past 10 years, PSAs have evolved from carve-out applications, such as medical directorship contracts, to what we continually refer to as "employment lite." While PSAs still invoke skepticism regarding their long-term viability, especially for hospitals/health systems, they are a viable and compliant affiliation structure. While not necessarily a preference of hospitals, they enable a practice to align with both a hospital and PE.

The evolutionary characteristics of PSAs as a full form of affiliation/alignment have resulted in the following key characteristics:

- **Continuation as a Long-Term Affiliation Structure.** When PSAs were first introduced, they were thought to be short-term, especially from the perspectives of hospitals and health systems aligning with medical practices. Expectations were that the arrangement would be for three or fewer years before the physician would convert to full employment (see conversion to employment below).

  However, many PSAs have been renewed several times because they work, they are proven, and there are no implicit or explicit requirements that they discontinue or convert to employment. The successes of PSAs are due to the fact that they can be short-term, long-term, or permanent.
- **Conversion to Employment.** With the permanency of some PSAs in mind, many have also ultimately converted to W-2 employment. This is part of the reason we refer to the PSAs as "employment lite." PSAs work well for an initial period, especially when the parties involved need time to earn each other's trust. However, if trust is earned and the health system's benefits package is better, it is common to convert to employment.

  We emphasize that once employment becomes the model, it will be more difficult, if not impossible, to enter other forms of affiliation. PE affiliation and some joint equity ventures are more challenging to set up. Still, PSAs that convert to employment are foremost in the industry. We estimate that at least half to two-thirds of the employment-lite PSAs have or will soon convert to employment, as that is the preference of most health systems.

- **Total Unwind.** Employment-lite PSAs work, and they rarely result in a total unwind; the practice returns to a private state, assuming there are no restrictive covenant limitations, and does not seek another affiliation partner. It is easier to achieve a total unwinding of a PSA than is possible with other models because under the PSA, the practice has retained its professional entity. Even within a traditional PSA, converting and transitioning to a fully private state is achievable. It is easier than if the practice providers or a portion thereof leave employment to go into a private or otherwise aligned structure. A total unwind is typically not acceptable to health systems and hospitals; thus, their initial hesitancy to agree to PSAs.
- **Private Equity (PE) Included.** If a PSA continues, a corresponding PE transaction is still possible, although uncommon, largely because hospitals and health systems will not approve this type of affiliation. Under employment, it is impossible for the practice to align with PE without the employer health system/hospital agreeing. Rather, the hospital or health system would have to divest itself of ownership of the practice before PE affiliation would be considered.
- **PSAs for Limited Affiliation.** We have discussed PSAs as an example of full alignment. Some PSAs are for specific initiatives, such as an outreach clinic or co-management agreement, or service line management structures. PSAs work well for such structures, including clinical integration agreements.
- **Practice Management Arrangements.** Typically, PSAs entail the physicians remaining independent, with the hospital or health system overseeing administration via a management services agreement. Sometimes PSAs are structured in a reverse manner. There could be a practice management arrangement wherein the physicians and other providers are employed, but the management structure is through a contracted entity that is owned or partially owned by the practice but is managed and operated by the hospital. This arrangement does not allow for an easy unwind, but if, for example, the practice has some

ownership interest via a management services organization, that entity could continue to provide these services post-affiliation.

EMPLOYMENT

Employment is the other primary form of affiliation between hospitals/health systems and physician groups. Employment involves an acquisition of the practice (typically its assets valued at fair market value), then, after the usual asset acquisition structure (as opposed to purchasing the legal entity itself of the practice), all employees and providers are fully employed. Employment encompasses all facets of work, with specific limitations on outsider earnings and any other affiliations. (Sometimes, hospital-employers make separate approvals for these.)

Employment structures have also matured through the years. In the early 1990s, employment of physician practices by hospitals and health systems became commonplace, yet it was a challenging time for all, primarily because of hospitals' lack of understanding and expertise in how to own, manage, and operate medical practices. Likewise, physicians and advanced practice providers (APPs) had difficulty adjusting to the subtleties of working as employees of a hospital or health system.

Challenges for the hospital included the way employed providers operated, how they perceived and/or desired independence or autonomy, and economics, such as the providers' compensation. The challenges were so broad that many employment deals were not renewed; some were converted to PSAs (though rare). In short, hospitals offloaded their employment and ownership of practices, returning to the typical medical staff's working relationships. The few exceptions were some smaller PSA wraparounds.

While challenges still exist, the processes and structures are working for the most part, partly due to some innovative management and operational formations, as outlined here:

- **Group Practice Subsidiary (GPS).** This is a simple employment model and is often applied to a medical group that has a large number of providers, locations, and other variables. This model also has a mature management and administrative infrastructure that is competent to allow its own level of independence and autonomy day-to-day.

  The employer hospital has the final authority, but given the practice's ability to operate successfully, the hospital smartly leaves the practice alone, allowing daily operations to continue unchanged. Within the hospital's physician enterprise structure, the practice can act and operate as a subsidiary.

- **Network Model.** The network model was developed when hospitals realized they had to upgrade their employment structures and the way they managed and operated them. The physician enterprise, which may be a legally formed subsidiary, allows for clinical integration across practices within the network and a degree of overall uniformity relative to policies, procedures, and administrative management. The network model has proven successful, even though some practices within the network would prefer a GPS model, which would provide more independence.
- **Clinically Integrated Network (CIN).** A clinically integrated network facilitates many elements considered essential within such structures, such as efficient management, effective communication (both clinical and otherwise), and fair compensation. Qualifying as a clinically integrated organization has some specific requirements. All are achievable, especially when the practices are employed under the same umbrella. Those providers who are not employed and in private practices can also join the CIN as outside parties but are subject to the same compliance standards and requirements.

What Is Different with Employment

Some elements of employment have improved over the years as physicians and APPs have come under the employment umbrella of a hospital or health system. Such changes include:

- **Management of Employed Providers.** Hospitals have learned that managing and operating a medical practice is different from managing and operating a hospital, and apply proper management principles to both.
- **Leadership and Governance.** Physicians have more input on daily operations, management, governance, and leadership roles. While the employer-hospital is the ultimate decision-maker, allowing physicians to be more actively involved is beneficial. The lines of authority are easy to draw.

- **Compensation.** Compensation of employed providers by a hospital or health system has evolved. Gone are the days of huge base/guaranteed payments. Arrangements typically include some guaranteed pay along with increased compensation. This is total cash compensation (TCC) tied to economic incentives plus quality incentives, creating compensation structures that reward but also involve risks.
- **Ancillaries.** Ancillary services have historically been perceived as the property of hospitals under an employed setting. A compensation incentive tied to quality metrics and wRVU production thresholds mitigates the complexities, such as compliance risks, of paying physicians and APPs based on ancillary performance. Nonetheless, when we expand ancillaries and their discussions to encompass joint ventures and joint equity models, the interest in and fiscal viability of the opportunities for these services expand greatly.

PE DEAL STRUCTURES

PE has influenced the entire arena of affiliation options for healthcare providers. While a new dynamic, there are numerous examples within all specialties of workable relationships that have developed between physician groups and PE sponsors. Although health systems and hospitals have stayed on the sidelines, an affiliation structure among practices, hospitals, and PE is possible, although this structure could not include employment of a group of physicians, as their employment would not allow for an equity-related transaction with PE. Equity transactions are almost 100% applicable to PE deals. Therefore, a PSA among a physician group and a hospital could be overlaid with a PE affiliation for the group.

The types of PE structures among physician groups and other providers of healthcare run the full range of complexity, from simple to multifaceted. Simple transactions typically include the PE firm acquiring the assets of the practice and then employing the physicians. The derivation of value is based on an earnings before income tax, depreciation, and amortization (EBITDA) restatement. This pulls earnings into the EBITDA total by taking away physician compensation (the "income scrape"). Creation of EBITDA earnings is then completed as to valuation via a market-based multiple. The physicians receive a greater payment at closing than would typically be the case with a hospital/health system PSA or employment structure.

A model that could be emulated within a PE structure involves a hospital/health system and the physician group. We call this "PE-like" in the sense that the structure is similar but with a hospital/health system rather than the PE sponsor. Derivation of value through an EBITDA restatement is comparable, although usually not as great as the PE firm would offer. The popularity of this model has not increased and is rarely, if ever, applied.

Hospital affiliation and PE are possible, but realistically, hospitals and health systems are averse to physician groups affiliating with PE in any way. This does not mean that PE and hospitals and health systems cannot work together or are not willing to collaborate; they do, although it is tedious.

One area where PE deals can work well with hospital/health systems' alignment is the latter's affiliation with certain ancillary services. These are "wraparounds" to the basic affiliation structure of employment or PSA. PE is interested in affiliation structures that include joint ventures and other forms of ancillary services that generate additional revenue and profits. Therefore, sharing with hospitals and health systems is not especially popular, though it does happen. It seems to happen more recently, especially when considering that partial participation in these ventures is possible.

PE will continue to be a leading model in the coming years, although it doesn't suit everybody. It has both positive and negative aspects, which advisers and attorneys should point out to the group prior to their serious consideration.

Figure 4.2 provides a concise summary of comparative applications of PSAs in the context of descriptive scenarios. The figure summarizes how the viability of PSAs compares to a full-fledged PE transaction, but even more to a hospital/health system employment scenario. The legend at the bottom of the figure is simple in that we have assigned a "+, -" evaluation for each descriptive item and how PSAs compare to other models. Unsurprisingly, those other models primarily focus on hospital/health system employment.

While Figure 4.2 focuses on the authors' experiences in actual application, others may agree or disagree with the evaluation assessments tied to the legend. Nonetheless, all 30 of these descriptive applications are relevant and should be a part of the decision-making relative to the strategy for affiliation pursued.

FIGURE 4.2. PSAs vs. Other Models in General*

Description	PSAs – Comparative +/-
1. Long-lasting relationships	+ -
2. Hospitals preferred	- +
3. Compensation	+ -
4. Compliance requirements	- +
5. Leadership/governance	- +
6. Benefits	- -
7. Staff employment	+ -
8. Administrative processes	+ -
9. Unwind ability	- +
10. Hospital bureaucracy	+ +
11. Deal flexibility	+ +
12. Physicians at greater risk	- +
13. Practice independence	+ +
14. Complexity greater	- +
15. Employment segue	+ -
16. Payer contracting	- +
17. Ancillary participation	+ +
18. PE affiliation possible	+ +
19. Financial security	- +
20. Variable PSA models	+ +
21. Employment negatives	+ +
22. Reporting protocols	+ -
23. Physician retention	+ -
24. Physician recruitment	+ -
25. Clinical quality	- +
26. Revenue cycle management	- +
27. Wraparounds viability	+ -
28. Quality metrics	+ -
29. "Full" integration	+ -
30. TCC effectively structured	+ -

*"Other models" include PE affiliation and hospital/health system employment with a significantly greater emphasis on the latter.

Legend

- \+ + Elements of both comparatively successful
- \- + Clearly PSA advantaged
- \- - Somewhat comparable – slightly PSA negative
- \+ - Clearly PSA negative

SUMMARY

Our approach to the discussion of the various affiliation models has been less focused on explaining the actual models, as they are widely understood. Instead, we have delved deeper into how these models are applied under the key areas of "full" integration/alignment/affiliation. These areas include PSAs, employment, and PE affiliation. We address merging groups in greater detail in later chapters.

With this foundation, in the next chapters, we will continue to consider other key traits of affiliation strategies in today's healthcare environment.

CHAPTER 5.

Health Systems' Attitudes

THE ATTITUDES AND PERSPECTIVES of hospitals and health systems toward physician integration and resulting affiliation transactions have evolved through the years. Many changes have occurred over recent years, ranging from relatively minor nuances to more significant deviations. Breaking down the major models and how those changes have affected each one is the theme of this chapter.

Affiliation transactions — such as professional services agreements, employment arrangements, or private equity deals — have become standard, making it less common for physician practices to remain independent and privately owned. We recognize that physicians still want privacy and autonomy. Many physicians, especially specialists, are even more determined to remain independent and autonomous from hospitals, health systems, PE, and others, even though they see the value in some limited or moderate forms of affiliation.

PSA RECEPTIVITY

As previously discussed, PSAs in the context of what we refer to as "employment lite" have become a definitive alternative to hospital and health system employment. Gone are the days of having to prove their legitimacy from an operational, financial, and compliance perspective.

The real question about PSAs revolves around what form of PSA exists. The global PSA, where the entire practice stays outside of ownership/employment by the hospital or health system, is often desired but less often agreed upon. The reasons include concerns about compliance, particularly related to revenue cycle management and "ownership" of the accounts receivable and related billing and collections processes. Many hospitals take a conservative and adamant stance on controlling all revenue cycle management functions, plus payer contracting. In these instances, a traditional PSA is likely the only structure that a hospital/health system will accept. There could be some acceptance of a carve-out PSA, where the hospital owns the revenue cycle functions.

Traditional PSAs are similar to employment. Figures 5.1a and 5.1b sum up the similarities between hospital employment and traditional PSAs and global PSAs. We illustrate those points carefully and thoroughly to show the similarity between these models. Thus, at the end of the review process, both sides (hospitals and practices) agree to an employment arrangement, if not immediately, in the not-too-distant future.

FIGURE 5.1a. Similarities Between Hospital Employment and Traditional PSAs

Employment	PSA
Highest level of integration.	Comprehensive affiliation strategy requires less integration than employment.
Hospital purchases all practice assets, including all ancillaries.	Multiple options, such as hybrid models, allow for a greater level of customization.
Practice entity dissolves and is absorbed by hospital.	Practice entity retains its structure.
All practice staff and physicians become employees of hospital.	Practice physicians remain independent.
Practice physicians gain stability but lose some independence and autonomy.	Hospital strengthens service line while practice realizes some financial/ operational benefits.
Provides easy segue to clinical integration and value-based strategies.	Offers easier segue to clinical integration and value-based strategies.

FIGURE 5.1b. Similarities Between Hospital Employment, Traditional PSAs, and Global PSAs

	Employment	Traditional PSA	Global PSA
Physicians Employed by Hospital	X		
Physicians Employed by Practice		X	X
Staff Employed by Hospital	X	X	
Staff Employed by Practice			X
Real Estate Owned by Hospital	*	*	*
Real Estate Owned by Practice	*	*	*
Non-Ancillary Medical Equipment Owned by Hospital	X	X	
Non-Ancillary Medical Equipment Owned by Practice			X
Ancillary Medical Equipment Owned by Hospital	X	*	*

(figure continues)

FIGURE 5.1b. Similarities Between Hospital Employment, Traditional PSAs, and Global PSAs

	Employment	Traditional PSA	Global PSA
Ancillary Medical Equipment Owned by Practice		*	*
Hospital/Hospital Affiliate Physician Benefit Plans Utilized	X		
Practice Physician Benefit Plans Utilized		X	X
Hospital/Hospital Affiliate Billing Tax ID Used	X	X	X
Practice Billing Tax ID Used			
Hospital/Hospital Affiliate Retains A/R (post-alignment)	X	X	X
Practice Retains A/R (post-alignment)			
Managed Care Contracting Negotiations Completed by Hospital	X	X	X
Managed Care Contracting Negotiations Completed by Practice			

**Depends on negotiated agreement.*

Once a medical practice forgoes daily management of the practice, particularly the revenue cycle management, there is little else for it to assume. The only possible exception is that continuing to employ the practice administrator and some departmental clinical staff would extend to a PSA. Thus, the traditional PSA is a logical segue to full employment. Giving up the administrative infrastructure is essentially the result of moving from a traditional PSA to full employment.

Carve-out PSAs, usually led by the hospital or health system, are also popular, especially when undertaking a new venture. For example, hospitals rightfully look to outlying service areas, where the socioeconomic status of a particular new area is growing and calls for their presence. In such instances, a carve-out PSA that focuses on that new area, with the hospital investing in a clinic location and other support services, is needed.

Physicians, both primary care and specialists, are reticent to assume any risks of moving into a new area, incurring significant start-up costs, and realizing inadequate revenue, at least initially. Carve-out PSAs, therefore, may focus on the physicians providing the professional services and the hospitals incurring all costs of administration and management, including revenue cycle and payer contracting. This mirrors a traditional PSA, but again, it may only be structured for that new carved-out clinic or other healthcare service. This arrangement has worked well in most instances.

Other forms of affiliation can be structured within PSAs. Often called "wraparounds," they entail additional agreements that are in support of and complementary to full affiliation, including employment, but more to employment-lite PSAs. Clinical co-management, service line management, medical directorships, etc., are wraparound strategies.

Finally, joint equity deals can also be considered a form of wraparound, but often are standalone investment opportunities for physician partnering. They provide equity that entails ongoing earnings distributions and enterprise value for that joint equity initiative. Of course, these transactions require much care and consideration regarding compliance boundaries.

So, PSAs have stood the test of time. Once regarded as "outside-the-box" thinking, they are now accepted and respected for their application and value when working with hospitals and physician groups and integration/affiliation strategies.

Numerous compliance restrictions must be followed, and we encourage engaging legal counsel to ensure those requirements are met.

EMPLOYMENT VERSATILITY

In recent years, hospitals and health systems have embraced greater flexibility within their employment of physician models. These models essentially prioritize independence and autonomy, even under an employment setting. While ultimately the employer is responsible for adhering to human resource and personnel policies along with treating employees well, this independence has grown to the extent that more hospital/health system employment models are allowing considerable practice autonomy.

When physicians entered employment arrangements 30 years ago, the structure was rigid. Hospitals had their employment model and varied it little. The limited variances were manifested in the contractual employment agreements and day-to-day operations. Physicians were resistant to such treatment and, coming from their own private practice setting where they were accustomed to making day-to-day decisions, found it to be a particularly challenging adjustment. Moreover, the hospitals were notoriously inflexible in their management style in that they believed the relationship with physicians was comparable to the operations of their hospital facilities, particularly the inpatient services. Nothing could be further from the truth as a "best way" of managing physician practices under an employment model.

Over time and largely due to dissatisfaction of physician employees, along with millions of dollars of financial losses, this paradigm shifted. Today, hospitals recognize that management operations and ownership of medical practices are not analogous to those of a hospital department or entire facility. True, there are some likenesses, and those should be recognized, but day-to-day, the operations are quite different.

This conclusion called for not only a change in paradigm but in attitude and overall functionality as well, wherein many hospitals granted physician practices a more overt management. On a direct basis, the result has been greater independence and autonomy for physicians in all areas: operations, financial management, and, of course, clinical delivery of services. It also relates to a structure that allows for more independence.

One such structure is the group practice subsidiary (GPS) model, which is constructed so that a mature, well-run, successful practice can remain a standalone entity within the hospital's physician enterprise. Therefore, independent day-to-day oversight is allowed, with the ultimate understanding that the hospital as employer has the final say. So, the GPS model looks and sometimes is legally structured as a subsidiary of a larger entity of the hospital. This model has proven successful in addressing the issues and challenges faced in original employment model structures in the 1980s and 1990s.

Another accomplishment/improvement in hospital/health system employment models is the ability for carve-outs and specific unit management. We previously discussed carve-out PSAs and how they are structured. Employment carve-outs have similarities and primarily allow for separation, dedicated to an outlying clinic as a new initiative, even a new ancillary service that the practice provides within a traditional employment model. Allowing specific carve-outs mitigates risk (just like they do with a PSA) and yet allows the hospital an opportunity to expand into new areas, new services, etc.

LIBERALIZED TERMS

Under employment, the original structures were standardized, using the same methodologies of compensation, governance, leadership, and overall structure. Most employed practices of hospitals were part of a large physician enterprise, wherein as much as possible, the operations, policies, procedures, and even the conduct of the physicians, were similar from one subset or practice group to another. While some consistency is good, extreme rigidity does not work (now or historically), and the sooner hospitals recognize this fact, the faster they work together with physicians in a successful manner.

So, there are opportunities under employment models to enhance not only the working relationship between physicians, APPs, and their hospital/health system employers, but also to allow greater independence and autonomy previously unrecognized or permitted. While the hospital, as the employer, is ultimately responsible, many responsibilities and duties can be allowed or delegated to remain within a historically successful practice operation. Even though all staff and all providers are employed (technically as W-2 employees), they can have the freedom to function.

GOVERNANCE AND LEADERSHIP STRUCTURE

As employment continues to be the preferred structure by hospitals and health systems, physicians and especially those who are part of a long-standing, well-managed group, have longed for greater ability to exhibit their management expertise and thus work day-to-day somewhat independently from their hospital employer. To their credit, hospitals have recognized this characteristic and have greatly improved their receptivity to and allowance of such styles.

Management and leadership do not have to be within a separate legal entity owned by physicians. To enable greater leadership under an employed structure, hospitals may allow independence and autonomy, while still having ultimate authority over a practice. Wherein they employ all staff and providers and have purchased all assets, the final responsibilities and decision-making rest with the owner of the business (i.e., the hospital/health system). Day-to-day, independent governance is the preference.

Decision-making is not surprisingly a key point of discussion. Who makes the decisions, both operational and daily, plus those that are higher-level strategic, longer-term in their impact? The answer is that hospital/health systems that are owners/employers, as well as solid physician management and leadership, should contribute. The final decision rests with the owner of the business, as it does with any other business.

We have noted on many occasions that the management and operations of physician practices are different, especially when hospitals are the owners. Even more important is the fact that hospitals and health systems have historically had a poor record in running, operating, and managing medical practices. One reason is their original refusal to allow physicians and their administrative leadership to take on daily leadership and management roles to make real decisions as opposed to being figureheads.

Another consideration is the make-up of the physician enterprise within the hospital and health system. The term "physician enterprise" infers that a separate legal entity (or a separate division or department of the hospital) that employs and/or contracts with physician practices to allow independence and autonomy among various physician entities is still possible. Even if it is less efficient to have myriad physician practice subsets within the physician enterprise, this arrangement is often important as opposed to merely having them under one legal umbrella. There can still be common policies, procedures, and overall management processes that allow some day-to-day independence along with an attitude of collaboration within major decisions.

For example, a well-established practice and its physicians should have input about whether to move or expand into a new location or facility, as the physicians likely know how best to structure and even to physically relocate to a new facility. Even though the physicians are technically employed and no longer have ownership, this partnership can and usually does work well.

Co-management and service line management duties and responsibilities also affect the subject of leadership and governance. Again, just because a physician group is employed does not mean that the physicians have nothing to add relative to their overall service line management and oversight within a hospital and health system.

Orthopedic practices, for example, whose providers have chosen to become employed, add much value to the entire musculoskeletal service line of the hospital. In fact, within many such settings, the orthopedic group is the primary service provider of musculoskeletal services for the entire hospital. Not allowing them input and some direct oversight over the entire service line is a mistake.

As service line and clinical co-management become more popular, there is the concern of the physicians "taking over." With proper guidance, management, and most of all, collaboration, this should not be a problem.

Similarly, dyad management works well. This type of management is typically structured so that under a service line management agreement, a physician group (or perhaps a single physician leader) works in concert with the administrative executive over that service line.

Some hospital administrators fear that if they allow more leadership and management emanating from a physician base or the physician enterprise at large, these providers will eventually "take over." This issue is easily mitigated with proper documentation of role responsibilities, job duties, and lines of authority. Ultimately, the hospital and its board leadership and governance structure will assume these roles.

Sometimes, when they have abdicated their responsibilities, physicians step in and assume perhaps more than they would otherwise need to take on. This is often a result of a lack of ownership and assumption of duties by the hospital leadership itself.

So, leadership, governance, and good management should be in play when a hospital or health system works with its physicians and defines not only the affiliation structure, but the duties and responsibilities of the employed and/or contracted providers. Those executives are ultimately responsible for that physician enterprise.

JOINT EQUITY STRUCTURES

We touched on joint equity earlier, but it calls for further consideration in the context of hospitals and health systems' attitudes toward management and operations of physician practices and other related healthcare entities. Real estate ownership is a prime example of how hospitals and physicians can work together to maximize their "partnership." Investments that physicians make in real estate are made privately and not as employees; it is almost always a separate legal entity and should be.

Everything structured within a real estate transaction must be at arm's length, with no exclusive deals allowed to the physicians. Such deals can easily convert into a compliance issue if not managed properly. Physicians must pay fair market value for their investment in such entities. With all these things in mind, however, real estate, whether a medical office building or raw land that is developed later, can be an excellent way for affiliation to have a long-lasting and successful effect.

Ancillary services can also be a part of the collaborative effort. While somewhat more challenging from a compliance standpoint (see Chapter 13 for further discussions), ancillary services have become more a part of the equation for all affiliation models pursued and developed between hospitals/health systems and physicians.

With compliance issues navigated properly through competent healthcare legal counsel, the process of expanding those ancillaries into joint initiatives that have a legitimate economic return based on the fair market value (FMV) investment by the physicians is win-win. Of course, ancillaries will vary with the specialty and should be consistent with the services provided within a particular specialty or service line.

Structured joint ventures (JVs) are also a part of this strategy. Specific to an initiative that fits the service line and overall operations, a JV is just that: a jointly owned entity when both parties (hospitals and their physician partners) have risks with specific investments involved. Such investments often require borrowing or otherwise finding some form of capital, and not just "sweat equity" contributed by the physicians (although some could be appropriate).

COMPENSATION VARIABLES

Without question, whether it's employment, PSA, or somewhere in between (such as with joint equity/JV initiatives), compensation and return on investment are key areas to consider carefully. The structure and methodology of compensating those involved, both administratively and clinically, is a major point of consideration.

Depending on the relationship structure, the compensation can vary, and the methodologies for computing the compensation are likewise varied. For example, under an employment model, the compensation is straightforward in that it will come under the "W-2" parameters, wherein the employed provider performs job duties consistent with their experience and ability and is thus compensated appropriately.

Ultimately, total cash compensation (TCC) is subject to state and federal tax withholdings and other related employee benefits and employee contributions. The "stack" of compensation components must be consistent with FMV and commercially reasonable totals. If not, a compliance issue is undoubtedly the result. Thus, it is essential to consider compliance issues as a part of the understanding when a provider/physician is employed by a hospital or health system.

Under contractual arrangements, FMV is applied and fully applicable. The various stacks of compensation should be considered, and employed contractors are just as much subject to the compliance boundaries as W-2 employees. All these issues must be taken seriously, or there may be compliance adjustments. Providers do not accept such adjustments well when they think that a compensation structure has been agreed upon and is ready to be implemented.

No matter what the model, health systems' attitudes toward compensating physicians have evolved over the years. Gone are the days of a guarantee of a significant percentage of the TCC. More plans today have a combination of some guaranteed income, especially if the physicians and other providers are employed, but more so, significant productivity incentive. Usually, the incentive is tied to wRVUs, which are much preferred over collections, charges, or anything akin to actual monetary value. wRVUs can be converted easily into compensation dollars, assuming the use of an appropriate conversion rate.

Quality incentives have been popular for several years, especially since the passing of the Affordable Care Act into law. Now, there are more compensation plans (again, both PSA and employment-entailed) that include a pool of dollars tied to quality outcomes. The metrics established for quality payments are a combination of certain performance standards and outcomes data. Usually, quality metrics are set up jointly by the physicians and the health system to accurately measure the things most relevant.

Leadership, both administratively and clinically, is also recognized and is often paid at a fixed rate per hour or unit of time spent on the completion of such duties. The duties are outlined based upon a proper job description, whether clinical or administrative, or even a combination thereof.

Ancillary services can also be a source of income, although they have more compliance risks and overall considerations. Nonetheless, they are popular as discussed earlier in this chapter.

Benefits and other perquisites are popular as well. Benefits, of course, are only applicable under an employment setting. Under a PSA, the value of benefits can be recognized and paid, but not the provision of actual benefits such as health insurance, life insurance, disability insurance, retirement, etc. Often, benefits or the lack thereof under a PSA are a determining factor in the decision of the providers to become employed rather than continue under a PSA. The benefit packages are more lucrative when employed by a health system that employs thousands.

Finally, group incentives are a part of the compensation structure under many models. This can work for both PSAs and employment, especially when the latter continues to be managed and operated as a unit (a group practice in and of itself). Group incentives can be tied to productivity, quality, and other individualized factors.

OVERALL FLEXIBILITY

On an overall, overarching basis, hospitals and health systems have matured a great deal, no matter their model of employment, PSA, or other forms of affiliation. Much more flexibility and openness toward collaborative thinking, planning, and even compensation structures are now the common approach for hospitals and health systems. This was not the case when hospitals first began employing physicians in the 1990s. Then, hospitals paid a guaranteed income and goodwill dollars upfront. Now, the only significant money paid upfront is for tangible assets, possibly the employee workforce in place, and supplies.

When looking at a possible offer, physicians are encouraged to consider the full package, but most of their "value" will be recognized through a more lucrative and thought-through compensation plan. While income from compensation is taxed at ordinary income tax rates (as opposed to capital gains rates), in the long run, if the employment or PSA term is lengthy, the value tied to the compensation is similar to the value that owners of private practices seek and obtain from their operations. In other words, they distribute all excess earnings to the partners via bonuses, which are also taxed as ordinary income.

Thus, the current flexibility is not more than even in terms of both economic and non-economic issues. This greater flexibility leads to greater satisfaction for both sides: the employer hospital/health system and the employee provider.

FREQUENTLY ASKED QUESTIONS

As we consider trends in hospitals' and health systems' affiliation strategies, several questions frequently arise. These questions and corresponding answers should help hospitals and employed or contracted physicians decide whether to move forward with such affiliation implementation efforts.

1. Are full alignment models necessary?
No, they are not necessary, but in many instances, they result in better working relationships and economic opportunities for the employer health system and employee provider. Keeping compliance requirements in mind, these opportunities have resulted in much better structured and more satisfied participants.

2. Is complete affiliation ("full integration") between hospitals and physicians inevitable?
No. While it is true that many (particularly younger) physicians have concluded it is best for their careers and practice to integrate fully with a local/regional health system, this is not always the case, nor do we believe it will eventually become such. Lesser forms of affiliation (see Figure 4.1) in every situation should undergo review, based on their specific merits and overall considerations.

3. Do hospitals need physicians to survive?
Yes, physicians are the key to any successful health system.

4. Is it best to align via "limited" or "moderate" forms of integration?
This depends on the individual situation. Some practices want more limited forms of affiliation, as they prefer to continue functioning as a private entity. In considering alignment options, the history and overall performance of the practice must first be evaluated, and the amount of integration determined. There are other factors in the decision of the best level of affiliation. These should all be analyzed with an open mind. Hospitals should respect the physicians' point of view and vice versa.

5. Should hospitals allow joint equity transactions with physicians?
Absolutely. This solidifies the relationship and allows for genuine interest and success, albeit within appropriate compliance boundaries. Increasingly, hospitals realize the value of joint equity ventures with physicians. These do not always have to be within clinical delivery services. For example, real estate is an excellent way to develop long-lasting relationships through partnering efforts.

6. Should hospitals allow private equity involvement?
This is a more difficult subject because PE will often want the physician practice to invest in other areas of collaboration, such as ancillary services. Hospitals do not welcome such investments, but three-way partnerships are possible and result more often as practices affiliate with PE but still want to work with their hospital partner. Turning a deaf ear to any form of PE involvement, whether in the practice or in the hospital and health system, is a mistake, as PE is a viable option. It does not work for all, but it can be positive for many.

7. Does a hospital mitigate certain economic terms by employing physicians/providers or contracting with them via PSA models?
Yes, these structures allow physicians to realize their value, often through a long-term agreement, whether it be employment or contractual. Various incentives are proper if the total stack of services and compensation is within FMV and commercially reasonable. Joint equity transactions can help as well, but are not always viable or received as well by hospitals, especially when they are compensating the physicians/providers on a productivity (usually wRVU) basis.

8. How sustainable are the current hospital/physician affiliation structures?
They are sustainable, having stood the test of time. However, they do require ongoing review, accountability, and adjustments. Therefore, they can be positive as to long-term affiliation but do require a fair amount of regular scrutiny. This entails both economic and non-economic terms and conditions.

9. Should hospitals overtly commit to only certain structures of affiliation?

We recommend a pluralistic approach. No one size or structure of affiliation fits all. Hospitals and health systems might entertain a variation of affiliation options, yet prefer certain ones. As such, hospitals that are narrow in their affiliation options or too concerned about whether certain "outside the box" thinking will hurt future deals should not be alarmed or concerned about compliance. Always having highly competent healthcare legal counsel to make sure that there is no structure askew from compliance standards is key to the pluralistic approach.

10. Should hospitals establish a physician enterprise to house their physician practices?

This is not a requirement; however, most hospitals have such an entity, whether they call it a physician enterprise, a subsidiary, or a network in tow. This allows for consistency of policies, procedures, and points of view. Having a common platform provides some economies of scale for expense control. The physician enterprise can vary and often does, with subsets of it being standalone, especially for highly successful practices that came as a unit from private structure to hospital employment or PSA.

The physician enterprise is the key vehicle that allows physicians, hospitals, and health systems to function with a degree of independence and autonomy. In other words, the physician enterprise is not a direct component but a subset of the hospital. It is a critical part of the overall hospital services, but it operates differently from hospital departments. Hospital-based physician practices can benefit from being a part of the physician enterprise, with some independence, autonomy in management, and leadership.

11. What works best for physician compensation post-affiliation?

Post-affiliation physician and other provider compensation is one of the most important components of any alignment structure, not only because of compliance requirements, but also for good fiscal management and oversight. So, the compensation structure is best served by variety. For example, guaranteed pay that makes up virtually all TCC is usually not the best. Physician incentives are essential.

The compensation "stack" is also important, as it entails a variety of methodologies and incentives to deploy. These help the physicians and other providers stay focused on their day-to-day functions, both clinical and administrative. Having a system in place with different forms of compensation, including certain bonus structures, is healthy. It allows for longer-term commitments. Some guaranteed income is wise and often needed to complete the initial transaction and compete as well.

12. Should a hospital place its PSA and employed physicians at risk?
Some portion of compensation should be at risk. At risk, though, can be as simple as hitting historical work RVU totals and then receiving compensation for an overage over a certain baseline. Other related matters include requiring physicians to fulfill medical directorships and service line management roles, and keeping these issues at the forefront of all areas of need and improvement. Having a partner to focus on is beneficial for all.

13. Should hospitals bundle (or even unbundle) payment components to physicians?
The compensation structure for employed and/or contracted physicians, from "limited" to "moderate" to "full" forms of affiliation, should undergo careful review. The concept of "stacking" is clear: each part within the "stack" is considered directly or indirectly. These would be separated and considered directly within the compensation structure. Indirectly, they may not be quantified as compensation for each part, but overall, all such components are considered to ultimately derive the proper compensation at FMV and commercially reasonable standards.

14. What model works most efficiently for governance and leadership?
A dyad model in which physicians and administrators co-lead a service line or subset within their respective specialties is an ideal structure for governance and leadership. If not a dyad model, allowing the physician group to manage its own infrastructure, even under employment or PSA, is advisable. Allowing physicians greater independence and autonomy has, in our view, been the single greatest area of improvement over the past 10 years. Hospitals have started to "get it" by allowing their physicians to take on leadership roles and to have a genuine voice in day-to-day operations and strategic planning. While not the ultimate authority, physicians have much to add and can do so in such a structure.

15. Would most hospitals be better off aligning only on a limited or moderate basis?

There is no right or wrong answer. In fact, there is no answer. It varies with the individual situation. It may even vary over time with the same practice and health system. Nonetheless, consistency in the application of alignment and integration forms, structures, and even economic terms is advisable. Having some variety is still the best decision.

Hospitals and physician groups are looking for these ingredients in today's affiliation structure, strategies, and overall make-up. Thus, continuing along the lines mentioned above of a hospital and health system implementing a pluralistic approach to affiliation applies here as well. "One-size-fits-all" does not work in this case. Independence with some degree of continuity, albeit legal structure and ownership under an employment model and full alignment through a PSA, works well in such settings.

16. Should hospitals limit their network?

Hospitals that continue to have opportunities within certain specialty practices should accommodate alignment. Hospitals should not be stymied by their forms and structures of affiliation due to a lack of adeptness at administrative functions. They must improve and allow the physician administrative leadership to assume more roles and responsibilities. Growth and expansion are needed in most settings, as many opportunities remain unrecognized or unexplored.

17. What is an acceptable "loss" of a hospital-physician enterprise?

This question is difficult, if not impossible, to answer. Opportunities for a network of physician practices to partner, some times long after the initial leadership of the practice and hospital are gone, make for an interesting longer-term working relationship. Therefore, it is imperative to consider and thoroughly discuss these matters in the first transaction. Any misunderstanding in this regard will only hurt the relationships, perhaps permanently.

With the above noted, there is no such thing as "acceptable" loss in the context of losing money on any venture. Nonetheless, "acceptable" loss has been known to be the actual loss, subject to certain service limitations, including timing thereof, with the owner. Working diligently together, hospitals and providers can turn the operational results around. Even if they operate continuously at a loss post-transaction, reducing it to a minimum is usually "acceptable."

18. Is antitrust a relevant issue to consider?
Yes. The purpose of antitrust laws is to prevent a competitive advantage due to an inordinate market share. This advantage may be a result of entities coming together as a single service. While our experiences within healthcare warrant relatively little concern, unless it is a major merger of healthcare providers, this still calls for careful review by competent legal counsel prior to any affiliation transaction.

19. Should APPs be of equal significance in such affiliation strategies?
Yes. APPs are relevant and valuable to the overall integration strategy of hospitals and physician groups. They provide essential professional services, complementing the physicians. Their transactions require similar scrutiny, review, and overall consideration.

20. Are primary care physicians (PCPs) a primary source of affiliation?
While certainly important, even essential, PCPs are not the only component of physician services that apply to affiliation transactions. Specialists of all types and expertise are equally important and should be considered accordingly.

21. Should hospitals fully align with surgical specialties? Which ones are most relevant?
Surgical specialties are essential to hospital services. Two specialties typically found in smaller hospitals and rural settings, general surgeons and orthopedic surgeons, are foundational and economically essential to maintain the viability of the smaller, usually rural, hospital. Moreover, these specialists requiring greater affiliation with hospitals, often via PSA or employment, are more in need than ever before. Recruitment and retention are huge hurdles for these facilities; thus, employment or PSA has become essential.

22. How best should hospitals market their aligned practices?
Whether practices are aligned through contractual relationships or not, hospitals should market every specialty, plus primary care, based on the services they provide. Thus, it is not a decision about whether to market, but rather about which services are tied to specific service lines within the hospital. Promoting market awareness of physicians' abilities, experience, track record, and reputation is proper and a good strategy.

23. Should hospitals have a documented recruitment policy?
Yes. Recruitment is an area of support for hospitals that can garner independent private physician practices. Certainly, hospitals can also recruit to employment or PSA in the fuller forms of such affiliation. Having a recruitment policy, sometimes including income guarantees, is also of great benefit and should be documented and updated regularly.

24. Should hospitals be amenable to nonclinical joint ventures?
Within compliance boundaries, this is a good strategy. An example is real estate, where physicians invest their own capital into a development such as a medical office building or some other healthcare-related facility. Such affiliation promotes the partnering attitude and yet must be at arm's length with no "sweetheart" deals offered to the physicians.

25. Do hospitals need medical staff affiliation near or long term, or both?
Some form (or more likely, forms) of medical staff affiliation that runs the gamut from "limited" to "moderate" to "full" (see Figure 5.1) is essential. A pluralistic strategy is essential for hospitals and/or health systems.

26. Should a hospital have a near-term and longer-term strategy for physician affiliation?
It should. This strategy is essential for all providers, and the better the strategic affiliation plan is documented and regularly updated, the better the benefits will be.

27. Do all compliance issues need to be considered in all affiliation transactions?
Yes. Compliance with government and other regulations is not optional. There are no exceptions.

28. What is the best way to educate physicians who want affiliation transactions about the various models and structures?
Physicians have varying degrees of understanding. Therefore, it is essential to explain and educate beyond the basic facets of the models and structures. Physicians and APPs should understand that factors such as compliance and limits on compensation are integral to the employment or PSA or otherwise affiliated strategy. Thus, fundamentally, when a physician group

aspires to hospital affiliation (or PE or merging with other practices), it is essential to engage a competent, independent adviser/consultant to educate and explain the nuances of the various models. Eventually, the return on investment of this extra cost will limit the questions, misunderstandings, and other negative outcomes that could otherwise result.

29. Is there a set compensation, operations, and overall infrastructure plan for affiliation in place? Is the due diligence and valuation process intact?

These are fundamental and essential components to any affiliation strategy, whether the strategy of the buyer or the seller. Such levels of understanding, education, and documentation are imperative.

30. Should a hospital align with a medical practice to avoid having to establish a joint venture with them?

No. JVs should stand on their own but can and should be a part of the overall affiliation strategy, as noted in various responses above.

SUMMARY

We have explored in some detail hospitals' and health systems' attitudes toward affiliation models and structures. More specifically, our focus has been on current-day trends, strategies, and tactical approaches to affiliation. Much has changed in the last few years, and while the models remain relatively constant, their application and variation across hospitals and health systems have driven the level of discussion here.

Physicians and other providers who participate in the professional side of healthcare services have become knowledgeable about the affiliation models. For example, many physician groups now understand PSAs ("employment lite"), and PSAs are more popular than ever. They are therefore still somewhat adamant about being the selected model, at least at the outset of the affiliation relationships. As we continue to consider the nuances of affiliation strategies, we will use this chapter as a foundation for better understanding and application.

CHAPTER 6.

Professional Services Agreements Versus Employment

As affiliation options have continued to mature, especially between hospitals/health systems and physician practices, the overarching models of choice are either professional services agreements (PSAs) or employment. In this chapter, our discussion of PSAs pertains to "full" affiliation, often referenced as "employment lite." Employment is often connected with W-2s while PSAs are connected with 1099s.

As discussed earlier, PSAs have become a legitimate and compliant option. They always were options, but their application and popularity have necessitated greater attention to ensure compliance with the parameters. Employment has existed for decades, as hospitals have provided staff-model structures for their physician enterprises. This "W-2" employment scenario addresses many concerns, albeit obstacles for physicians, especially those recently out of training. These physicians do not have to worry about day-to-day operations, infrastructure, management, or, to some extent, financial performance.

Thus, the options of PSAs versus employment are clear and often addressed by the physician groups and hospitals/health systems as fundamental when a practice expresses a desire to align fully.

As a result, we submit the following overarching assumptions relating to the discussion of PSAs versus employment:

1. We assume that PSAs are legal and can be established and administered in compliance.
2. Not only are PSAs within compliance boundaries, but they also entail similar forms of compensation and performance requirements as employment.
3. PSAs are part of the hospital/physician enterprise and can be used as a full form of affiliation, with no other limits on the length of the agreement.

4. Employment remains the preferred model, especially for hospitals and health systems. And while it is not required that PSAs convert to employment, they are a legitimate and often applied segue.
5. Fair market value (FMV) and commercially reasonable (CR) compensation are no different under a PSA than under employment. Both require careful scrutiny and validation within fiscally sound and regulatory requirements.
6. PSAs and employment can therefore have similar compensation incentive structures.
7. While there are some inherent differences between PSAs and employment, there are more similarities than differences.
8. PSAs provide a structure for practice physicians who want to be independent and "private." As a result, the physician practices engaged with and affiliated with hospitals through PSAs can participate in other activities, such as providing services such as ambulatory surgery centers, unless contractually prohibited.
9. Employment entails inherent restrictions: Once a physician or APP is employed, it is difficult, if not impossible, to engage in other outside activities and/or contracts with independent provider entities. Thus, employment is more confining.
10. PSAs have the capability to include carve-outs and hospital-based contracts (e.g., for anesthesiology, radiology, inpatient services, etc.).
11. The differences between PSAs and employment are based on the type of PSA (i.e., traditional versus global versus practice management arrangement).

With these overarching factoids under consideration, let's explore in much more depth these two forms of full affiliation and how they are best applied in today's hospital, health system, and private physician medical practice services.

SIMILARITIES BETWEEN PSAs AND EMPLOYMENT MODELS

Fundamentally, a PSA is subject to the memorialization of specific services of a professional nature that are performed by the physician and/or APP for a hospital or health system. While PSAs could apply to physicians working for a for-profit healthcare provider offering imaging, surgical, and other services (i.e., not a hospital, per se), our focus is mostly on PSAs between physician groups and hospitals. Therefore, we refer to previous examples and the detailed discussion regarding descriptions of PSAs in this context. Traditional or global PSAs are usually the primary alternative, though in some cases, practice management arrangements and other variations of PSAs are considered.

Nonetheless, keeping things somewhat simple, the following list summarizes the similarities in the key areas of consideration between PSAs and employment.

PSA versus Employment — Similarities — Key Areas of Consideration

1. *Pay Structures*
   - **Description:** PSAs are often confused with requiring different pay structures from employment. Similarities of structures and traits include fair market value/commercially reasonable compensation dollar limits and compensation "stack" limits.
   - **Success Strategies:** Applying the same analysis as for employment will often yield similar successful results.
2. *Incentive Compensation Metrics*
   - **Description:** Several components of incentive total cash compensation (TCC) include:
     - Productivity incentives often tied to units of production such as wRVUs.
     - Quality incentives tied to clinical performance outcomes, etc.
     - Wraparound compensation forms, such as clinical co-management and service line management.
   - **Success Strategies:** These incentive models have proven to work comparably to those in employment and offer excellent incentive opportunities for the PSA-contracted provider.
3. *Recruitment and Retention Efforts*
   - **Description:** While some limitations may exist on how much a health system can assist, recruitment remains an option for the private group.
   - **Success Strategies:** Recruitment guarantees are for private practices. Thus, those under a PSA are appropriate. Retention efforts are

often more effective within PSAs because of the practice's private nature and its appeal to physicians.

4. *Term of Contract*
   - **Description:** PSAs and employment agreements have defined term lengths, usually with the option to extend.
   - **Success Strategies:** Similar terms between employment and PSAs have resulted in long-term relationships. Some PSAs have converted to employment over time and continued through extended generations.
5. *Termination Rights*
   - **Description:** PSAs and employment agreements entail similar termination rights. Often, both agreements can be easily exited, with 90 days' prior written notice.
   - **Success Strategies:** Flexibility in termination, along with some agreements that have similar, more stringent, and strict termination rights, applies to both PSAs and employment agreements.
6. *Real Estate*
   - **Description:** Real estate investments may be structured under both employment and PSA affiliation models. As such, these investments are separate and thus managed at arm's length, unrelated to the actual clinical affiliation model.
   - **Success strategies:** The ability to recognize other forms of mutual investment (i.e., partnering in real estate developments) when managed separately from the clinical and other forms of affiliation has proven to be successful in the long term.
7. *Revenue Cycle Processes*
   - **Description:** Whether PSA or employment, the hospital and/or health system preferably assumes payer contracting, billing, and collections of professional fees' duties. This allows a level of ownership and authority, no matter whether it is a PSA or an employment model.
   - **Success Strategies:** Notwithstanding the challenges many hospitals face in billing for professional services by physicians and APPs, this process has proven more successful for many hospitals. This especially applies to payer contracting rates, where hospitals can usually receive better reimbursement per unit of service than physician groups.

8. *Coding and Documentation*
    - **Description:** Whether a PSA or employment, the provider physician and APPs must code and document accurately.
    - **Success Strategies:** Few differentials have resulted in coding and documentation based on the type of model, whether PSA or employment. Proper compliance and related controls still prevail, regardless of the structure.
9. *Governance and Leadership*
    - **Description:** The terms and conditions for governance and leadership between PSAs and employment should be similar. While PSAs entail the practice being a private entity, there can still be crossover duties and responsibilities given to the physicians within a PSA. Moreover, dyad management between the hospital and the physician group has proven successful.
    - **Success Strategies:** Allowing physicians leadership and governance roles within the physician enterprise makes no difference, whether PSA or employment. Both models accommodate such. It is recommended that physicians be allowed significant input in these roles. The understanding that the hospital employer (and even the contracting hospital under a PSA) is ultimately in charge still prevails, no matter the model.

DIFFERENCES BETWEEN PSAs AND EMPLOYMENT MODELS

The differences between PSAs and employment models can vary from transaction to transaction. The independence of the PSA model and how that reflects upon the overall relationship is a core variable. The following list summarizes the differences in the key areas of consideration between PSAs and employment, with a focus on PSAs.

PSA versus Employment — Differences — Key Areas of Consideration

1. *Autonomy and Freedom*
    - **Description:** Most PSAs allow some independence and autonomy, enabling the practice to align with others besides their primary PSA

partner. Some PSAs restrict physicians from aligning with others, even under the PSA.

- **Challenges:** Allowing a private practice to affiliate with any other party is onerous to hospitals and health systems and will often result in a halt to any further negotiations without some level of exclusivity being granted to the hospital. As a result of stronger wording relative to outside investments/partners, the PSA may be much more restrictive, almost identical to those restrictions under employment.

2. *Benefits*
   - **Description:** The provision of benefits is reimbursed within the PSA model and therefore is workable. Traditional PSAs in which hospital staff is employed mitigate this concern, as all non-provider employees participate in the hospital's usually more lucrative benefit program.
   - **Challenges:** The PSA requires benefits for the providers, and possibly all staff, and creates challenges relative to the economic value of the overall payment. Hospitals are reluctant to pay higher benefits costs when they could employ both providers and staff and provide benefits at a lower cost. This may be a reason not to pursue a PSA and, thus, direct all attention to an employment model.
3. *Other Strategic Opportunities*
   - **Description:** Akin to point #1 above is the allowance under PSA models for physicians to consider other strategic opportunities, such as ancillary services, ambulatory, and imaging centers. Syndication of ownership in ancillary entities may be offered under a PSA or employment, but the latter is becoming more prevalent.
   - **Challenges:** Other opportunities pose a direct competitive threat and are usually not allowed by the hospital under the PSA agreement. Some strategic opportunities may be allowed, such as investment in real estate and other investments less directly involved in healthcare. These strategic opportunities may be syndicated with the approval of the hospital or health system and could be within an employment model.
4. *Practice Assets*
   - **Description:** The assets are still owned by the practice, which

allows for an easier unwinding of the PSA. The assets owned by the practice are leased and must be completed based on an independent valuation of the FMV of the leasing terms.
- **Challenges:** While an agreement for the leasing of the assets and other related services usually can be effectuated, it is one more hurdle to overcome within a PSA, whereas under employment, the assets are purchased at FMV.

5. *Private Equity (PE) Affiliation*
   - **Description:** PSAs entail contractual ("1099") relationships between the practice physicians and other providers and the hospital/health system. Technically, this contractual relationship does not prohibit a PE transaction by the private component of the group. A global PSA results in a greater likelihood of a PE affiliation.
   - **Challenges:** Inherent to such an ability is the hospital and health systems' negative attitude toward PE. A negative attitude exacerbates resistance from hospitals or health systems; they will not allow the practice to affiliate with PE whether or not there is a PSA between them and the practice. Regardless, many transactions have been completed wherein PE is involved with the practice and the PSA with the hospital or health system. In other words, this is doable, but often a "deal killer."
6. *Cost/Overhead Variations*
   - **Description:** There are nuanced differences between PSAs and employment regarding overhead. This also may vary depending on the type of PSA. The traditional PSA calls for the hospital to be responsible for operations overhead, including non-provider staff employment. The global PSA casts this responsibility to the practice and is subject to a line-item budget reimbursed up to that amount. Another major overhead item that varies between these two models is employee benefits. Under a global PSA, all benefits are provided by the practice. Under a traditional PSA, only the provider benefits are absorbed by the practice. Under employment, all benefits are provided by the hospital. Finally, there may be additional costs incurred by the practice, even though employment and/or a traditional PSA result. These costs include legal fees that are attributable strictly to the practice, tax

preparation, and accounting fees, and related outside costs, even under an employment structure.

- **Challenges:** The variations in overhead present some challenges within a PSA model, as these costs are not reimbursed and must be absorbed by the practice; thus, they come from the funds paid by the hospital to the providers and/or the practice, depending upon the PSA structure. Legal and accounting fees, profit-sharing/retirement fund oversight, and administration are all costs that must be absorbed by the practice over and above their reimbursement from the hospital under a PSA model. This could be the case, even under employment, but for the most part, under employment, more such costs are absorbed by the hospital.

7. *Governance/Leadership Structure*
   - **Description:** The PSA allows for a more specific definition of governance and leadership responsibility. Because the practice is still outside of employment under the PSA model, governance and leadership of the practice are typically defined more broadly to maintain the separate relationship between the hospital and the practice. All this to say that the practice can more easily be representative of its interests and somewhat "across the table" from the hospital in such matters. This could also be the case under employment, but because the providers and all other staff are employed by the hospital, the tendency for broader representation in governance and leadership may be lessened as a result.
   - **Challenges:** While governance and leadership can still be structured to allow the practice/providers a significant contribution toward day-to-day management, this is typically less broad under employment. As an employee, the physician may feel somewhat inhibited in their ability to contribute to day-to-day governance and leadership responsibilities. The inherent arm's-length nature of PSAs allows more independence in governance and leadership duties and is thus often more effective.
8. *Practice Hierarchy*
   - **Description**: The hierarchy of management within the practice remains when a PSA exists because it is a private entity; under employment, this hierarchy is often dissolved. If left intact, much

will depend on the hospital's willingness to allow a separate structure to be maintained. Specific administrative leaders, such as president, vice president, or managing partner, plus a collective executive committee are typically part of the leadership of the private practice. This may be allowed under employment, but is less likely and ultimately is usually dissolved.

- **Challenges:** Under employment, the practice will be less likely to have its own management hierarchy, given the fact that all providers and staff have become employees of the hospital. PSAs, by contrast, are inherently characteristic of the practice hierarchy remaining and in fact being adamantly opposite to their hospital contractor/employer.

9. *Compensation Variables*
    - **Description:** Under employment, the compensation of the providers is more readily accepted by hospitals, whereas under the PSA, hospitals often view the compensation structure as akin to private entity negotiations. These structures should not vary between employment and PSA. Compensation must be at FMV and CR rates, regardless of whether it is employment or PSA. Another matter similar to compensation is billing and revenue cycle management. Under employment, the hospital is comfortable maintaining those processes. Under a PSA, hospitals prefer to retain control of the revenue cycle but may outsource some functions to the practice. Given their familiarity with managing their revenue cycle processes, it is often beneficial to allow them to continue their involvement in revenue cycle management. Payer contracting is assumed by the hospital, regardless of the model.
    - **Challenges:** Developing compensation and revenue cycle processes is potentially more challenging under a PSA. However, both are doable and should not be an overarching reason for employment over PSA. To be clear, from compliance foundations, FMV and CR should not waiver. However, if a hospital prefers to pay a physician more under employment (often the case) and that higher pay is within the proper pay range, it may legitimately offer more under employment or PSA.

PERCEPTIONS VERSUS REALITY

When evaluating the characteristics of professional services agreements versus employment, it's clear that many points are misunderstood or misinterpreted. Many of these misconceptions stem from hospitals' understanding of the PSA model and structure. When these misconceptions are addressed and resolved, the parties then move forward and agree to a PSA model or employment. Several common assumptions by hospitals and physicians are summarized below.

1. ***PSAs are more short-lived and easier to unwind.*** True and False. While some PSAs are of shorter duration, they do not have to be. Many PSAs have renewed several times and continue to be a largely successful "full" affiliation model. As for the unwind, PSAs typically are easier to unwind, although there may be terms in the PSA contract that make an unwind more challenging.
2. ***PSAs are easier to amend along the way.*** True. As an independent contractor agreement, there are less confining and restrictive terms and conditions than under employment. Moreover, PSAs allow for other ventures, although they sometimes are precluded by hospitals restricting them contractually.
3. ***PSAs and employment carry similar FMV and CR requirements.*** True. This is often misunderstood. Simply stated, fair market value and commercial reasonableness stand on their own merits and requirements and do not allow greater compensation of one over another. There is a difference in that the employer hospital may generally opt to offer higher compensation under employment than under PSA, both within compliance standards. This then becomes more of a negotiation rather than a compliance issue.
4. ***Physicians prefer PSAs; hospitals prefer employment.*** True. Physicians appreciate that PSAs allow them to remain in private practice yet be fully affiliated with a hospital. Hospitals prefer the control and general oversight, along with other areas of confinement characteristic of employment.
5. ***PSAs allow more freedom in decision-making.*** True. Because the practice remains private under the PSA structure, there is a tendency for that independence to be further manifested in greater independent

thinking. While employment can provide such independence, it is not as open and pervasive. The prevailing mindset among physicians and APPs is employment versus independence. PSAs are therefore often more viable, especially at the outset of a hospital-practice "full" affiliation.

6. ***Governance within PSAs allows for similar traits to those under employment.*** True. PSAs provide physicians and APPs independence and freedom of thought, as noted above. This transcends to governance, at least during the initial years of affiliation, as hospitals and practices are acclimating to each other.
7. ***Employment will, over time, be received by all.*** True and False. This will vary. Often, when a relationship starts with a PSA, the parties build a level of trust and confidence in each other that later leads to employment. Thus, the best long-term relationship for all, especially the hospital, is usually employment. But often, a PSA is the best way to initiate an affiliation relationship.
8. ***PSAs may transition to employment, but it is not inevitable.*** True. Many hospitals view PSAs as merely a stepping stone to full employment. Often, this is the case, but it doesn't have to be, as there are myriad examples of PSAs in third and fourth generations. Meaning the agreement has been renewed and extended several times.
9. ***Employment entices physicians to such a structure because hospitals often offer improved terms not agreed to under a PSA.*** True. To be clear, there should not be any difference in FMV and CR compliance terms or in specific rates between PSAs and employment. However, the hospital can choose to offer a better financial package for employment. Thus, if hospitals prefer employment (as they usually do), they may, as a matter of policy, offer better financial benefits (if they are still within those compliance boundaries).
10. ***Restrictions may be less for outliers, but these still exist in such transactions.*** True. No matter, PSA or employment, specific restrictions may be relaxed for outlying locations, practices, etc. For the time being, restrictions such as non-compete covenants will continue, even though the courts have indicated the potential for them to become unenforceable sometime in the future.

11. ***Ancillaries are easier to share and/or be participatory in jointly owned structures under a PSA***. True. JV transactions are possible under employment models. These are often effectuated via syndications (discussed in a later chapter) wherein the employed physician invests through the at-arm's-length syndication model. Generally, such cases are less common because the hospital increases compensation for the physicians under employment. Moreover, they insist upon retaining all ancillary services and their profits. Because of the continued private nature of the practice within a PSA, joint equity is more viable.
12. ***Payer contracting and ownership of the work RVUs corresponding to overall reimbursement plans and structures can work under either PSA or employment models***. True. But generally, payer contracting and the revenue cycle processes of resultant billings and receivables are "owned" by the hospital. This is preferred for PSAs and, of course, is the methodology for employment.
13. ***PSAs are relatively short in duration; thus, they may not stand the test of time***. False. While PSAs may be relatively shorter, they do not have to be. Through renewals and extensions, they can stand the test of time.
14. ***A health system that is amenable to both PSA and employment models will prevail over time much better.*** True. Hospitals and health systems that have adamantly said "no" to any form of employment-lite PSA have struggled, generally less successful within their physician enterprise. Deploying a pluralistic approach wherein both models are possible will inevitably yield better near-term and longer-term results.
15. ***PSAs allow the private group more latitude in the use of its resources, such as its facilities.*** True. Overall, this has been the case, as rental rates and the value of real estate should be no different, whether a PSA or employment. It is essential that rental rates, regardless of the model of affiliation, be at FMV. Allowing such versatility is best, as it will attract more practices toward affiliation and encourage them to seriously consider completing a transaction.
16. ***FMV and CR criteria are equally important, no matter the model.*** True. They are not only equally important; they are required.
17. ***Traditional PSAs are mostly preferred by hospitals. Practices more so prefer global PSAs***. True. Either model can and will work and be compliant.

18. ***Hospitals often place specific limitations on PSAs.*** True. These limitations include such things as:
    - A term length.
    - Intent to ultimately convert to employment.
    - Hospital controls the revenue cycle.
    - Hospital owns ancillaries.
    - Hospital employs the staff.
    - Provider-based billing may be a preference or a requirement of the hospital (this is generally not popular with the practice).

These are common characteristics, especially of employment-lite PSAs. While these perceptions are often close to reality, there are numerous areas in which both hospitals and physicians have misconstrued or misunderstood what is possible within both PSAs and employment. Thus, it is incumbent upon all parties to understand these characteristics and resultant nuances.

EXPLORING PREFERENCES

Hospitals clearly prefer employment. Many physician groups prefer employment-lite PSAs. Both are possible. Neither should be an adamant, insistent position. Pluralistic approaches are best, meaning that not all physicians or hospitals are best for employment. Many are not best suited for PSAs. Careful assessment should be completed, and a collaborative discussion should be held.

Often under the guidance of an independent adviser or consultant, the "best" model is obvious. With a fair evaluation of these options completed, the final decision of whether an employment-lite PSA or full employment will be made. Keeping an objective, open mind to both PSAs and employment achieves the best results.

Why Hospitals Prefer Employment

To summarize, here are the salient reasons hospitals prefer employment:

- Hospitals perceive, and often correctly, that greater control and long-term affiliation is best effectuated through employment.
- PSAs are often believed to be difficult to maintain long-term.
- Overall, hospitals can justify greater compensation under employment, even though both employment and PSAs are subject to FMV and CR requirements.

- Hospitals believe that employment allows them to more easily adhere to compliance requirements.
- Hospitals believe that technology is more adaptable under employment.
- Taxes are more predictable and straightforward under employment.
- Benefits are more compelling and overall, better structured under employment.

Why Practices Prefer PSAs

Practices prefer PSAs for these reasons:

- PSAs allow broader opportunities because the practices are still private.
- Practices view PSAs as being fully aligned but subject to less control by the hospital.
- Many physicians believe PSAs provide them with a greater voice in governance and leadership, due to their independent nature.
- Comparable pay is possible and still allows the measure of independence for physicians within the PSA.
- Generally, there may be fewer enforceable restrictions under PSA structures.
- Taxes may be better managed under PSAs.
- Overall, physicians, once they understand PSAs, believe the same alignment and integration opportunities exist between them and the hospital. Because of the ability to maintain greater independence, *et. al.*, they often prefer PSAs over employment.

SUMMARY

This chapter has taken the overall discussion of affiliation by PSAs compared with full employment to a deep level by pinpointing issues, perceptions, and flaws while accentuating the positive aspects of both models. The bottom line is that either model will work and maintain compliance; both can meet the goals and objectives of the employer-hospital and the physicians/providers.

CHAPTER 7.

Private Equity Model for Hospital–Physician Transactions

WHILE THE EMPLOYMENT MODEL has become somewhat the standard for full integration, this model continues to evolve in terms of structures and approaches. For example, private equity investors increasingly have an impact on healthcare market dynamics.

Although private equity investors are not new to the healthcare world, in the current marketplace, these actors stimulate change and evolution of the standard transaction structures and approaches to value creation. This activity, in turn, results in more change that trickles down to other players in local healthcare markets and the industry as a whole.

PRIVATE EQUITY INVESTORS AND THEIR IMPACT ON HEALTHCARE MARKET DYNAMICS

Before we go deeper into the private equity (PE) approach, we need some clear definitions. PE firms are investment fund providers that manage substantial amounts of capital (usually $100+ million to $100+ billion). The capital is procured from other institutional investors, such as global banks, hedge funds, high-net-worth individuals, and family offices. Some PE firms are diversified across multiple industry sectors, regions, and the like, while others have a more specialized focus, such as energy, natural resources, real estate, or healthcare.

The investment model behind most PE firms is to deploy capital into a targeted space by acquiring a platform company, which is typically the firm's entrance into a specific type of business, market segment, or region. Once this platform is stabilized and optimized to its fullest potential, it will function as a flagship with the primary focus being the launch pad for growth through add-on acquisitions made by the company. When an appropriate level of growth has been achieved, the PE firm is apt to pursue liquidity by selling the company to a buyer or through an initial public offering or another transaction.

There are two main points to this discussion. First, although we often refer to private equity transactions within the healthcare services space, many of these deals actually occur at the platform level. Second, the platform acquisition deal typically entails higher valuations and more flexible terms compared to what generally are more standardized and rigid models pursued in add-on acquisitions. This point is critical because in many cases, once the PE firm completes a platform acquisition and implements its operators to stabilize the business and begin pursuing add-on deals, the majority of PE deals are executed by operating companies that are owned by private equity investors.

Since PE investments are not new to the healthcare industry, why is all this discussion about private equity investors relevant to healthcare services entities? It is important to understand that healthcare is fundamentally a local business. Regardless of its structure, ownership, tax status, and players involved, the dynamic between healthcare providers — physicians and hospitals — is centered on local market dynamics.

Based on the current nature of healthcare services, the delivery of medical care not only begins and ends with but also revolves around clinicians and the organizations under which they operate, including medical practices, hospitals, and other similar entities. Considering this dynamic in terms of the standard hospital and physician practice, it is straightforward, albeit not always without some degree of complexity. However, when the dynamic of an outside party is added, for instance, a PE firm or PE-sponsored platform entering into a market with significant capital reserves and, in many cases, fewer regulatory constraints, this could substantially disrupt what once functioned as a relatively simple local healthcare market dynamic.

This scenario is what we currently see in many markets with PE firms entering and causing significant disruption. This perspective is not meant to cast a negative light on PE firms and PE-owned entities, which have the right to implement their model where it makes sense — in many ways, this might result in significant value creation and overall economic growth. PE investors are not big bad wolves trying to negatively affect local healthcare markets. Indeed, disruption can often result in significant value, as we have seen repeatedly in other industries.

The primary question is how healthcare provider organizations can continue to remain flexible and dynamic in creating value for their organizations as they confront this evolving market disruption.

THE PE MODEL AND COMPARISON WITH TRADITIONAL ALIGNMENT MODELS

While hospitals and physicians can pursue many alignment models, the most common transaction structures between these entities are a practice acquisition coupled with physician employment and professional services agreements (PSAs).

As many groups have considered options with potential buyers other than hospitals, there has been a significant increase in the number of deals in which practices sell to PE firms or PE-backed platform companies. These deals, however, typically involve vastly different structures and terms compared to hospital–physician transactions. Below are some of the common characteristics of these models:

1. **Hospital acquisition of practice, coupled with a physician employment agreement.**
    - Acquisition typically includes only tangible assets and, hence, minimal upfront money.
    - Practice can sell any ancillary separately at fair market value (FMV).
    - Compensation plan is based on individual physician production with some quality incentives.
    - Typically makes sense for primary care or practices where the priority is reducing risk and attaining more stability in income over upfront dollars.
2. **Professional services agreement.**
    - Practice maintains independence, but there is no upfront money because there is no sale of practice; tangible assets could be sold or, more likely, leased via the PSA.
    - Practice can sell any ancillary separately at FMV.
    - PSA rate is based on a group rate per wRVU; payments can be distributed by the practice.

- Typically makes sense only for surgical specialists or proceduralists where reimbursement has declined significantly and where ancillary reimbursement has decreased, such as cardiology.
- Surgical practices are more likely to have higher-value ancillaries (e.g., ASCs), which would allow for upfront dollars if those ancillaries were acquired.
- This essentially is the same as going to a single-payer contract where the PSA rate with the hospital becomes the sole source of revenue.
- While maintaining flexibility in how compensation dollars are distributed by the group, the practice still retains risk and overhead obligations through its maintained independence; other typical employment requirements, such as restrictive covenants, are in force.

3. **Private equity acquisition of practice.**
   - Upfront value (i.e., intangible value or enterprise value) in the practice is created through the application of a physician compensation reduction.
   - The compensation reduction ("haircut") is treated as newly created earnings before interest, taxes, depreciation, and amortization (EBITDA), which can then be applied in a discounted cash flow (DCF) model that determines enterprise value.
   - The haircut is permanent, so the physicians will make less income going forward; however, they would have received the value of that reduced income in the upfront dollars.
   - Some prospective offset to the haircut may be realized via improved access to services and organic growth.
   - The likelihood of the practice being sold soon or possibly experiencing other consolidation based on the new owner's preferences is high.

In the past, hospitals have been reluctant to pay significant upfront dollars to practices, and for good reason. Medical practices fundamentally have no intangible value, as they in effect distribute all their profits in the form of excess compensation to their physicians/partners. Because they distribute earnings to their physician partners as compensation, the FMV of a medical practice typically is limited to tangible assets.

This is a regulatory limitation for hospitals; however, it is not something that PE firms or private, for-profit corporate entities are required to follow. Still, they follow it for ROI purposes. (Note: The PE model also facilitates succession planning and, thus, is often more appealing to the older physician, five years or less from retirement.)

Recently, however, the perspective has shifted ever so slightly. Some hospitals have begun to explore whether they could pursue the same structure as PE firms in their acquisitions of medical practice entities. That means they will not change their position on paying significant upfront dollars tied solely to intangible value; however, hospitals could explore greater upfront money if those dollars were tied to something more tangible, such as the compensation haircut. This is sensible because until now, hospitals have been forced to stand by and watch as PE firms enter their local markets, write large checks, and then implement significant changes that have broader implications (and in some cases adverse effects) on the local healthcare market.

Also, there is a unique component as to how a valuation can be derived from this model that could increase the appeal for physicians to partner in this structure with the hospital over a PE firm (which we address in the valuation section below).

VALUATION CONSIDERATIONS AND KEY DEAL DRIVERS

Before we discuss the valuation in these transaction structures, we must first understand the key drivers of the deal from the perspective of the practice. In evaluating options from the practice's perspective, the most important initial question the sellers must answer is, "Why are they doing this?" More specifically, "What is their main priority to achieve in doing a deal?" The buyers must ask themselves whether the main priority for completing a deal is one of the following:

- Maximize upfront value.
- Accept lower upfront value in exchange for more stable income.
- Maintain income but reduce risk of reductions from CMS and commercial payers.
- Remove the risks and difficulties of running an independent practice.
- Maintain independence while still achieving greater income stability.

- Partner with another organization to increase opportunities for income diversity.
- Address the needs of succession with the practice.

If the consensus among the physicians selling their practice is to maximize the valuation paid at the time of the transaction and forego their independence to an outside organization (hospital or PE firm), then the PE model may be the best option. This favorability will increase if the practice is a primary care or a group with few ancillaries. This model likely is the only real option for maximizing upfront value for that type of entity; however, even with ancillaries involved, if the hospital is willing to purchase them, that will only increase the upfront value. Accordingly, this structure becomes even more appealing for surgical specialties.

So how does the valuation work in the PE model? It is a relatively simple approach, although significant technical analyses, modeling, and assumptions are required to derive an accurate dollar amount. In general, these are the key components of deriving enterprise value in the PE model:

1. Determine the haircut (i.e., compensation reduction) to be applied across all physicians.
2. Develop a pro forma financial model whereby the haircut ultimately is turned into EBITDA with growth over a five-year projection period. (Note: There are critical and detailed steps that must go into the development of these models; however, for this discussion, we assume the model follows all relevant and appropriate standards.)
3. Calculate a discounted cash flow valuation model using the financial tenets from the pro forma. This will derive an enterprise value for the entity following appropriate guidelines and standards.

Figure 7.1 offers a generic, high-level description of how this process works and relates to how the general numbers might fall. (Note: This is a hypothetical example and presented in general form using round numbers.)

In the example in Figure 7.1, each physician in the group would receive $2.25 million in upfront value for their practice (assuming the proceeds were distributed evenly), compared to the $250,000 in compensation relinquished each year.

This model also assumes the PE firm applied a multiple of 9x to the haircut amount to derive its transaction value. However, few true market

FIGURE 7.1. Example of Acquisition by PE Firm

Acquisition by PE Firm		
Practice Revenue		$50,000,000
Total Physician Compensation (Pre-Haircut)		$25,000,000
Total Number of Physicians		10
Haircut	10%	$2,500,000
Reduced Comp per Physician		$250,000
Multiple on Haircut		9
Transaction Value		$22,500,000
Proceeds of Transaction per Physician		$2,250,000

multiples can be applied to such deal models. As such, applying a multiple against the haircut to derive the value would entail a varied multiple in each transaction based on the financial resources, risk, and flexibility of the parties involved.

This valuation calculation would relate solely to the sale of the practice. If the transaction involved the sale of ancillaries or other related entities, such assets would be valued separately and ultimately add value to the sellers in those deals. Typically, the ancillary services would be a separate legal entity, such as an ASC, or for purposes of the transaction, would in effect be treated as such.

As noted, the standard approach for applying this model with PE firms is for the haircut to be a permanent reduction applied throughout the life of the post-transaction relationship to validate the upfront dollars. The PE investor requires this action to allow an adequate return on investment over a short period of time. Then, there likely could be another transaction or liquidity event soon after that.

PRIVATE EQUITY-LIKE MODEL FOR HOSPITALS

There are potential differences for a hospital pursuing a transaction with a practice under a PE-like model. A hospital's ROI can be factored in a variety of ways, and in most cases, it would not consider flipping the practice in five or fewer years, as a PE firm often does. Therefore, there is room for flexibility in the structure and economics of a potential transaction.

To compete with PE firms in such scenarios, hospitals must provide more upfront value than is the case with other models. A hospital cannot write the same size check to purchase a medical practice for as high an upfront value as a PE firm. However, they potentially could present a more appealing offer by implementing the haircut for a defined, limited period, such as three years. So, instead of the physician sellers receiving all their intangible value upfront in exchange for a permanent compensation reduction, they could pursue the same structure in which the upfront value is less than a PE offer (though still a significant amount), and their compensation is restored after a relatively short period.

Using the same generic figures from Figure 7.1, the hospital-driven PE model potentially could be as illustrated in Figure 7.2.

FIGURE 7.2. Acquisition by Hospital Using PE Model

Acquisition by Hospital Using PE Model		
Practice Revenue		$50,000,000
Total Physician Revenue		$25,000,000
Total Number of Physicians		10
Haircut	10%	$2,500,000
Reduced Comp per Physician		$250,000
Term of Haircut		3
Total Reduced Comp per Physician		$750,000
Multiple on Haircut		N/A
Transaction Value (under DCF Approach)		$19,125,000
Proceeds of Transaction per Physician		$1,912,500

In the example, the value of the practice was derived not from a multiple applied to the haircut but from a DCF model. This is a separate process that requires its own discussion to explain fully its mechanics and how a valuation is derived. However, it is a widely used and accepted valuation methodology provided it is implemented under the proper guidelines and standards. Nevertheless, the value of the practice paid through the upfront proceeds of the transaction is less than the value paid in the PE acquisition.

The more important distinction is that while the physicians received almost $1.913 million in upfront dollars, this amount was attained in exchange for giving up $750,000 of compensation over three years. After Year 3, though, the compensation is restored with appropriate increases, meaning the physicians would continue to benefit from the transaction going forward, more than if they had done the same deal with a PE buyer.

SUMMARY

In evaluating this structure, the consideration is what the physician sellers hope to obtain from a transaction. If they want as much money up front without concern for the impact on future compensation, then a hospital may not be the best option. However, if they seek a significant portion of the practice's value off the table via an upfront distribution of funds while maintaining the ability for this compensation to be restored in the future, the PE-like model could be attractive for both a hospital and the physician group.

CHAPTER 8.

Merging Practices

ONE OF THE MORE POPULAR strategies involving medical groups is merging with other like-minded practices. Merging two or more practices is no easier to complete than the other affiliation options, and perhaps it is even more challenging. In this chapter, we will devote our efforts to answering the questions that inevitably surround the options, alternatives, and reasons for pursuing mergers.

FREQUENTLY ASKED QUESTIONS

The typical questions asked about the alternatives surrounding mergers, as opposed to affiliating with hospitals and health systems and private equity (PE) firms, deserve comprehensive responses.

1. Why do practices merge? Mergers offer a viable alternative for medical groups, especially when they have considered PE and/or hospitals and health systems' affiliation previously. Further, once merged, the opportunity to align with health systems and/or PE increases. Mergers are thought to be a stepping-stone toward the ultimate strategy of hospital/health system or PE alignment.

Additionally, many physicians are more comfortable when affiliating with fellow providers. They engender trust, although typically, mergers do not involve a significant financial payout at the time of the actual consolidation. The merger may offer value for the future, but it clearly does not generate a financial windfall at the time of completion.

The concept of strength in numbers is often applied to mergers. To avoid the possibility of restricting trade and antitrust violations, the parties must give much attention to these laws. Nonetheless, coming together with a single provider number offers opportunities to work with other hospitals and health systems on potential affiliation models. Even payer contracting may be a resultant benefit.

2. What is the best way to structure mergers? There is no "best" way to structure a merger. The options follow a process that could begin with small combinations of operations that merely result in a single provider number consolidated into one legal entity for purposes of contracting and other day-to-day initiatives. Over time, that continuum of combined functions may entail full operational mergers, but this evolution is not a requirement. Often, combining operations yields the greatest financial savings in costs and overhead. These consolidations require substantial adjustment and reconciliation of operations, leadership, governance, and the like.

Therefore, the structure may evolve over time, or the merger's closing could be deferred until the time to address fully all key operations analyses, including governance, leadership, income distribution plan, etc. In short, there is no absolute right or wrong to the structure that is adopted. Obtaining an experienced advisory council (legal, tax, and consulting) is the best way to navigate these issues.

3. What are the key components of mergers? To be successful, the key elements are the issues that matter most to physicians. Examples of the components are the distinctions between the structural set-up of mergers and the issues to consider within them. All are essential factors to consider, deal with, and resolve prior to completing the actual legal transaction. Some post-merger issues can be deferred until after the merger closes, especially if the initial emphasis is on legally merging and then later, when considering the best way to combine operations, administration, leadership, and governance.

Nonetheless, the key components to considering and completing mergers are as significant as ever. Global issues that include the structure, operations, governance, financial terms, physical facilities, and clinical delivery are all major areas to reconcile and agree on prior to making any meaningful change in both legal structure and post-merger operations.

4. What mergers are easiest to complete? Typically, mergers are best completed in situations where the physicians have commonality in the services they provide, such as their specialty. Single-specialty mergers are usually easier to complete than multispecialty ones. The reasons are obvious, as multispecialty mergers entail a wide range of services and, to some extent, areas of focus in the delivery of clinical care.

Although there is no routine way to complete mergers, it is best to merge practices in a way that considers all the issues and reviews and reconciles many of the areas prior to closing. Some issues can be postponed until after the legal transaction occurs, but ideally, the major global issues outlined above should be addressed, reconciled, and agreed on first.

5. What are some of the obstacles to success? There are many obstacles to completing successful mergers. This is why we recommend that the key issues be reconciled prior to the actual merger event/closing. One example of such an obstacle is the combination of operations. Knowing when best to address these issues is key to a successful merger.

The concept of cost savings through "economies of scale" is a good example of how mergers can benefit the practices involved, but also can cause disappointment. Typically, those cost savings are not realized for some time, even for two to three years after the merger. In fact, in many instances, costs can go up for the first year or two after a merger. The cost of merging itself may be the culprit.

Other obstacles abound, from "culture" to clinical services output. Management and administration of the practices can also create friction. All these matters are critical to a successful merger and are also obstacles to success.

ECONOMIC DRIVERS

Not surprisingly, successfully merging medical groups and other healthcare services entities involves a substantial number of economic drivers. While economic improvement is not the only reason for a merger with another practice, it is among the top considerations. Often, in the face of a variety of obstacles, groups will continue with a merger under the auspices that the economic drivers are the most compelling reasons for consolidating. In other words, the economic benefits that the new entity attains in time are chief among the justifications for the merger and supersede other obstacles.

The key economic drivers of merging practices include the following:

- **Merging Overhead.** Economies of scale and consolidated overhead to eliminate potential duplicative costs are a key reason for merging. As we noted earlier, typically, the practices realize no financial windfall at the time of the merger; in fact, costs may increase for some time after the merger. Nevertheless, a significant driver for the merger is the opportunity to reduce or maintain similar overheads as a percentage of revenue.

- **Allocating Costs.** Spreading costs is another form of economies of scale and results in an effective overhead rate that is not higher and hopefully is lower, particularly as a percentage of total revenue. The concept of fixed costs being the prominent overhead component of medical practices applies. As fixed or mostly fixed costs are spread over a larger group of providers, the effective costs on a percentage and absolute dollar basis go down. Thus, allocating certain costs to the various components of the merged practices is a viable economic driver.
- **Revenue Growth Potential.** Merging practices should improve revenue. The various touchpoints include payer contracting reimbursement from commercial payers, spreading ancillary services over a larger number of providers to realize improved return on investment (ROI) on those ancillaries. (Downtime of certain ancillary services actually creates an opportunity cost that is mitigated when the downtime is reduced.) Revenue may also grow through the completion of more services within the practice, as the overall talent pool and the experiential nature of the providers are greater than they would be if they had not merged and acquired additional talent.

  Therefore, revenue growth is a genuine opportunity and useful for leveraging greater negotiating prowess with hospitals and health systems to secure services that the merged group may provide.
- **Enterprise Value.** While the total value of the enterprise (the merged entity) is sometimes overestimated and thus overvalued, it should be greater. Forming a platform of providers without the influence of PE but with the same principles is a key economic driver for merging practices. The concept of the sum of the parts being greater than the whole is at play. Several practices geographically spaced within an area offers greater potential for revenue growth and a better bottom line. This may be one of the most prominent reasons for merging groups. They have been careful not to violate antitrust regulations, but still cover a much broader area of services. The larger group also presents stronger negotiating capabilities, whether with commercial payers, hospitals and health systems, or in the future, PE.

OPERATIONAL CONSIDERATIONS

Earlier in this chapter, we considered in some detail the operational qualities of potential value in the merging of medical groups. The same principles apply when groups consider other forms of affiliation, such as hospitals or health systems and PE. Often, merging groups improves operational/administrative structure that, in turn, improves economic drivers, consistent with those discussed above. Characteristics of mergers and improved operations include:

- **Revenue Cycle Efficiency.** Managing the overall revenue cycle to limit contractual discounts, write-offs, and adjustments, and improving billing and collections are often positive outcomes of the merger. This effect should not be overlooked as a reason in and of itself to merge. Improving the central business office and, by extension, the general revenue cycle management is of immense value and should be a key objective of every merger.
- **Management Effectiveness.** While selecting the best administrative leadership can be difficult, given that the merging groups bring their own administrative management expertise, having the talent available post-merger is beneficial. Deciding who should lead the administrative operations of the merged entity is one of the most challenging issues and can be an obstacle to success. Nonetheless, the talent pool is much deeper, and while not all available talent is necessarily needed, those individuals who provide the best administrative support can be retained. Moreover, the merged entity can afford to retain this talent pool. Eventually, a deep talent bench leads to more effective, efficient management.
- **Negotiation Prowess.** We reiterate here that, in the context of operational improvements, the enhanced ability to leverage the merged talent pool to focus on improved, yet fully compliant, economic terms with hospitals/health systems and commercial payers is beneficial and valuable. Indeed, this may be the best reason for merging operations (as opposed to a legal-only merger structure).

STRATEGIC DRIVERS

Like affiliation strategies for medical groups and hospitals/health systems and PE, when considering mergers among medical groups and related healthcare service entities, there are several critical strategic objectives.

These are drivers to complete the merger and are often worth reminding all those involved, as challenges and obstacles present themselves. The following points discuss these key strategic drivers:

- **Payer Contracting.** While it is essential that all efforts be made to eliminate antitrust challenges, the ability to consolidate resources in a legal manner vis-à-vis the merger process is the most important goal and objective of a merger. The legal structure is possible without merging operations; however, previous discussion indicates that payer contracting is also a major economic and strategic driver.

  Payer contracting with commercial payers is a major opportunity, albeit a challenge, for all private practices. Without the backing and overall expertise of an affiliate partner, such as a hospital or health system, it is difficult for private groups to negotiate the best contractual rates. Moreover, when mergers occur, rates do not increase automatically. Thus, even before the merger closes, research and analysis should be completed to support the overall premise of increased reimbursement rates due to the "strength in numbers" structure.

  It is difficult to measure to what extent payer contracting rates might improve due to a merger, which adds to the risks involved in moving forward without knowing the full impact of increased reimbursement rates, if any, post-merger. Nonetheless, the greater number of providers under a single federal identification and resultant billing account should enable that merged entity to experience a rate comparable to that of any one of the merging practices. The objective is for everyone to experience some increased reimbursement rates. Again, we emphasize the need for thorough due diligence analysis pre-merger to determine whether this is a possibility.
- **Hospital Relations.** Medical groups led by physicians with the support of advanced practice practitioners (APPs) should not enter a merger with other groups on the premise that they can completely absolve any relationships, working or otherwise, with applicable hospitals. On the contrary, hospitals need physicians and vice versa. Just because groups merge and become a stronger voice with their affiliate hospitals does not permit those groups to abandon the support and overall services they provide at their current hospital(s).

That said, the same principles discussed above apply under payer contracting. That is, the merged group, now much larger with a stronger voice, has opportunities to improve on its economic and strategic working relationships with its hospitals within appropriate compliance boundaries. Continuing to be a part of the medical staff and exercising talents and abilities to be within the hospital's leadership ranks as members of the medical staff is immensely valuable and should not be overlooked. Within the merger process, the larger merged entity has more to offer in terms of talent and services; thus, their merger may result in an overall improved working relationship.

- **PE Potential**. Merging into a larger group is often a premeditated and intended precursor to the merged entity completing an affiliation with PE. A merged entity is much larger and offers more ancillary services, which is attractive to PE. Further, the inherent efficiencies often come with an ability to provide more skilled administrative talent. The platform for other acquisitions is of great interest to PE and often offers opportunities to achieve a higher total enterprise value, which offers greater net value to the investors and the physicians.
- **Ancillary Services**. Whether the merged entity proceeds with a hospital or PE affiliation, the merger should result in greater capital from increased profits due to revenue growth, cost containment, and other measures. This increase enables the merged entity to expand the ancillary services it provides to its patient base. Often, the merged entity can raise its own capital to fund ambulatory centers and other ancillary entities. While hospitals or PE may not welcome increased ancillaries, this capability can serve as the key component for meeting the objectives of physician affiliation strategies without selling out to PE or a hospital/health system.
- **Benefits Enhancements**. A medical group is often driven to affiliate with a hospital/health system or PE because of the group's lack of benefits and/or their high cost, even within a merged group, but certainly with the non-merged private group. The merger facilitates more total lives covered by health insurance and other benefits. Consequently, it is a strategic driver for affiliation, especially when groups are not yet interested in hospital or PE alignment. Overall, the purchasing

power of benefits is improved by the larger merged entities' ability to spread those costs.

- **Critical Mass.** A larger-sized merged entity can plan for even more impressive and larger investments, such as real estate/medical office buildings. Whether or not these are established within separate entities (typically our recommendation), they are closely aligned with the merged medical group and thus a part of the overall strategic plan for the merger.

  Without this critical mass, many of these things could not be done or would require greater risk exposure for fewer physicians. Larger numbers also enable the physician owners to offer equity participation with key non-provider employees, including administrative leadership. This participation enhances both recruitment and retention of the best talent in those areas.
- **Recruitment and Retention.** Whether it's administrative staff or providers, a merged entity with greater revenue and profits is more able to recruit and retain personnel. The new entity can hire more competent, experienced talent to run, manage, and operate their ventures. Likewise, the nature of the merged entity promotes longevity and retention.
- **Growth Potential.** The matters noted above enhance the potential for revenue and profit growth. This growth would not be possible or highly unlikely if the merger of such groups were not completed.

These strategic drivers should be included within the documentation, both before and at the time of a merger's closing. They should form the basis for articulating and following through on the goals and objectives post-merger. Providing this documentation and adding the timelines and milestones expected to be achieved, post-merger, will enable the newly merged entity to achieve more success.

MERGER SNAGS

In many cases, merging financial operations, services, and cultures among the groups may kill the merger altogether. Thus, being aware of likely snags is critical. Moreover, being objective and realistic about the severity of these snags is essential to overcoming them. Merging groups is a major undertaking for everyone involved, entailing significant time and capital. The viability of a merger should be determined as soon as possible. One way to help determine whether a merger is fundamentally possible is to bring in an experienced and objective adviser/facilitator to guide the process. This step is money well spent when approaching such a weighty decision.

The following is a list of the complications that are obstacles to mergers based on our experience.

- **Income Distribution Plan (IDP) Challenges.** Often, the merging groups have different income distribution plans for their partners and employed providers. As a result, structuring a plan that accommodates all merging providers is challenging if the structure of the IDP is not considered early in the merger negotiation process. In that case, it could be more than just a snag but a prohibitive roadblock that prevents the merger from occurring.

  For example, some IDP structures call for equal sharing of the profits of ancillary services. The strength-in-numbers concept applies, where practices (post-merger) can deliver more in ancillary profits, including the utilization of costly equipment that produces additional margins. Some merger structures allow practices to have some continued uniqueness, such as in a pod model with each pod having its own IDP.

  IDP snags are often the major reason smaller groups do not join in a multi-group merger. In addition, multispecialty group mergers create many challenges in the efforts to have a consistent IDP across the post-merger structure. Addressing these snags requires compromise, give-and-take, and readjustment. We recommend careful consideration of the IDP formula post-merger, with a thorough explanation of the new IDP.

- **Leadership and Governance.** Groups that are merging have their own leadership and governance structures, and typically, like the IDP, they are reticent to make changes after the merger. Nevertheless, a common leadership and governance structure post-merger is essential. All partners entering the merged entity should have equal rights, including voting and representation in the governance and leadership structure.

  Although structures vary, usually a board or executive committee will be formed, comprised of representatives from all merged entities.

While it is impossible to have equal representation, especially if the merging groups have varying numbers of physician partners, the expectations should be that all merged groups have some direct representation and that each group be fairly represented in the voting process for the leadership of the group. An independent adviser can help with the structuring of the governance and leadership post-merger.

- **Management and Administration.** The expectation within each group often is that their administrator is "the best" person and should direct the merged group. The best policy is to find job responsibilities for each group's administrators as appropriate and cost-effective. Defining the management infrastructure, both physician and non-physician, is another imperative that should be discussed and resolved before the merger ensues. Postponing these decisions will cause significant disruption, disagreement, and possibly cause the merger to "blow up."
- **Asset Contribution.** Each practice contributes its assets to the merged entity. The value and actual totals of those assets, from equipment to furniture and other tangible items, will vary. Thus, the question is whether the merged entity accepts the contribution of these assets without economic reconciliation. In this event, each group simply contributes its assets, and the expectation is that each physician partner has equal ownership in the post-merged practice.

  The alternative is to determine the value of those assets contributed and create some reconciliation to allow for an equal share. This decision would require some financial payment to the practice for those contributing a greater value of assets. In a merger process, we typically do not recommend pursuing this path.

  A simpler solution is for each participating practice to receive no remuneration for any excess contributions. Otherwise, the financial ramifications of trying to equalize contribution values is impossible.
- **Strategic Planning.** Each of the merging parties should understand and agree on whether they want to take their post-merger group funds strategically. Without an agreed-upon strategic plan, the merger's success will be minimal.
- **Locations.** A merger usually entails practices that overlap in physical facilities and locations. Often, the physicians are owners (or part-owners) in the real estate and/or the practice has a long-term lease that

is financially dependent upon the practice's lease. The practice must continue as an independent entity, servicing the lease via monthly rental payments.

Such snags can disrupt and even terminate the merger. Thus, where possible, even if over a limited period, the merged entity should honor all leases from its participating practices. It is often possible for the merged entity to take the space initially post-merger, with the understanding that as soon as realistically possible, certain locations will be subleased to outside parties, with any shortfall on the lease being offset.

Therefore, there are ways to address the location-overlap issue, but the additional costs that often result must be considered in the post-merger pro forma. It is unfair to ask a practice to take a monetary loss on a lease or some additional real estate responsibility solely because of the merger.

- **Differing Cultures.** Cultural issues are the most undefined of all the potential snags, but without question, they create the most problems. Defining culture in and of itself is a challenge, but essentially it is the way the physicians and staff conduct themselves day-to-day, the things they prioritize within their practice, and the feeling (or lack thereof) that exists of a somewhat small business/family atmosphere.

  Culturally, these challenges should be recognized early on, and like all the other potential snags, a reconciliation should occur. Although each group's culture continues, an effort to work within the new culture of the merged entity should take precedence. Having an outside adviser help evaluate the culture issues and recommend the best way to merge the varying cultures is the way to move forward. It is essential that the varying cultures blend as a unit.
- **Hospital Affiliations and Variations Thereof.** Merging several groups often entails addressing varying hospital relationships and affiliations. Careful analysis, review, and evaluation of the hospital affiliation is necessary pre-merger. Hospital affiliations for the newly merged group are worthwhile to the extent that the larger group can cover multiple hospitals (vis-à-vis competitive issues), which enables greater opportunities. However, the competitive element where Group A has worked with Hospital X and Group B with Hospital Y, both within the same service area, could involve a significant roadblock. The merger

should proceed, but it may take away from financial and related affiliation structures with one of the two competing hospitals.

- **On-Call Duties.** Once a group is merged and in a similar context to multiple hospital affiliations discussed above, on-call responsibilities will likely result in roadblocks toward the merger. Overall, physicians view on-call responsibilities as somewhat onerous and, as a result, issues covering both the practice's admitted patients plus the patients entering via the hospital's emergency department must be reconciled prior to merger closing.

SUMMARY

We have considered both positive and negative aspects of the issues related to merging practices, absent a hospital or health system full affiliation model, and most likely absent PE. Merging practices can be a viable solution as an alternative to hospital integration and/or PE affiliation. Despite the challenges that must be addressed, merging groups can be a viable strategy for affiliation.

CHAPTER 9.

Clinical Integration Update

CLINICAL INTEGRATION IS A RESULT of an overt collaborative initiative primarily focused on healthcare providers (hospitals/health systems, physicians, advanced practice providers, etc.). It is structured collaboration that coordinates care across the continuum of healthcare services within that legal entity, encapsulating clinical conditions, settings, and improvements focused on quality and efficiency, especially cost efficiency. In a clinically integrated network (CIN), the member providers participate in joint sharing of clinical data to improve care coordination and clinical quality.

CINs must demonstrate through proper mechanisms and vehicles that they utilize technology, have a shared understanding of how clinical services are coordinated, and that they can do so. In turn, the CIN may qualify as a "provider network" that enjoys reimbursement from the payers and distributes that reimbursement to the applicable individual providers.

The lengths required to prove clinical integration are due to its serving as another form of affiliation among providers and payers. It is a formal entity, it requires capital to implement, and it is a definitive alternative to other models discussed in this book.

CLINICAL INTEGRATION PROGRESSION

The concept of clinical integration and clinically integrated networks can be traced back to the early responses to the Affordable Care Act, which was signed into federal law in 2010. Since then, several changes have taken place including:

- **Antitrust guidance reset.** In 2023, the Department of Justice (DOJ) and Federal Trade Commission (FTC) withdrew longstanding healthcare antitrust policy statements going back to the 1990s, and then with the 2010–2011 ACO statement.[1,2] CINs are no longer viewed as "safety zone" entities, with joint contracting tied to clinical integration now being assessed on a case-by-case basis under the rule.
- **Clinical integration and CIN expansion.** CINs increasingly depend on interoperable data exchanges and near real-time analytics. As

such, their infrastructure has matured, and qualified health information networks (QHINs) have been established. Their establishment enables better standardization, with clinical data being exchanged among network members, and improves a core prerequisite of clinical integration.

Quality and cost efficiency are still the primary drivers. The framing of these requirements has evolved from a mere contracting vehicle to a performance platform. Physicians often lead the governance process with appropriately transparent performance measurements that frequently dictate reimbursement. Payer negotiations typically hinge on these documented enhancements.

VALUE-BASED REIMBURSEMENT

Clinical integration and CINs are tied mainly to value-based reimbursement (VBR). While other forms of payment may be part of the CIN entity, including fee-for-service (FFS), quality and value-based models are typically the means for paying providers within the clinically integrated structure.

As such, some recent adjustments have put VBR front and center with the concepts of clinical integration. For example, in 2021, 35% of Medicare Advantage and 24% of Medicare FFS plans incorporated the concept of alternative payment models (APMs).[3] These APMs are at the core of accountable care organizations (ACOs) and CINs, which are normally tied to non-governmental affiliations (somewhat akin to ACOs being tied to government reimbursement and CINs to non-government reimbursement).

Recent surveys have substantiated that most payers expect APMs to grow, and an overwhelming majority believe APM expansion will improve care, quality, and coordination.[3] APMs with downside risk have also increased, with 28.5% of total U.S. healthcare payments flowing through APMs with downside risk, increasing from 24.5% only three years ago.[3] Provider sentiment has also improved in that in early 2025, 40% of medical practice leaders had a positive outlook on value-based care, 40% were neutral, and 20% were negative.[4]

How do these statistics mesh with CIN strategic trends? CINs are increasingly focusing on readiness for risk-based contracts, including expanding into specialty-driven, episodic-based total cost-of-care structures.[5]

As a result, all players, including providers, payers, government, and possibly even U.S. healthcare consumers, are starting to buy into the concepts surrounding reimbursement for *quality* and *value*. At the core of the commercial side of this dynamic are CINs and clinical integration in general.

How the landscape will evolve is still uncertain, but with each passing year, a clearer vision among payers emerges, with at least partial reimbursements based on quality and value derived, along with cost controls and care coordination.

How does this affect affiliation models? Affiliating through and within a CIN is still a legitimate strategy of affiliation, although it would be structured more as a wraparound to the core model of affiliation, such as employment-lite PSAs, employment by hospitals and health systems, and PE alignment. Having the ability to be clinically integrated is thus important.

CORE FUNCTIONS OF A CIN

As CINs and their related ACOs continue to evolve, they have become a core structural model for affiliation. Therefore, they are an option for medical practices and hospitals, as well as some private investor entities and possibly even payers, to consider within their overall strategies for affiliating with physicians. CINs have evolved in recent years, as detailed here:

- **Evolution of Governance.** CIN governance structures in recent years have included PE-backed physician groups, digital health companies, and expanded roles for physicians. In other words, CINs have not depended exclusively on hospitals or health systems to exist. The capital typically needed for CINs is large enough, however, that hospitals have been the principal partner, supplying much of the start-up and ongoing capital required. PE has the capital and has, in some instances, replaced hospitals and health systems (or they have chosen to work together). Nonetheless, the capital required and investment by PE-backed companies must have a clear intent and strategy for a return on that investment.
- **Advanced Data Analytics.** AI-driven population health analytics and predictive modeling have progressed dramatically in recent years, enabling the CIN to more effectively identify high-risk patients and manage chronic disease.[6] CINs, therefore, have assumed a more

sophisticated role in the continuum of affiliation models, particularly in relation to reimbursement from payers.

- **Standardized Clinical Protocols.** At the core of clinical integration is the ability to better coordinate care plans and overall delivery, inherently improving quality at no greater (and hopefully less) cost. The broader adoption of evidence-based care pathways, supported by real-time performance dashboards and quality reporting tools, is a hallmark of CINs.
- **Interoperability Enhancements.** Interoperability has always been a key component, although it is not always realized. With the introduction of QHINs, standardized and secure data exchange has been achieved across all CIN participants.[5] Secure interoperability should be a core characteristic of CINs.
- **Social Determinants of Health (SDoH) Integration.** Many CINs now embed SDoH screening and community research referrals in the care coordination processes.[7]

All these innovations have contributed to the maturation of CINs and have lent considerable support to their viability. Still, much capital, organizational structure, and realization of value are needed and often lacking. Thus, other forms of affiliation (more direct affiliation) are usually preferred, with the CIN being a wraparound.

REGULATORY CONSIDERATIONS

Not surprisingly, CINs continue to come under intense scrutiny regarding regulatory compliance. Lack of proper compliance could terminate their existence or significantly hamper their ability to function effectively. Therefore, it is essential to enlist competent expert legal counsel to ensure regulatory compliance. Areas of concern include:

- **Requirements.** The DOJ and the FTC withdrew their legacy healthcare antitrust policy statements in 2023.[1] This paved the way for CIN joint contracting to be assessed on a case-by-case basis under general antitrust law.[2] Nonetheless, CINs must demonstrate substantial clinical integration, measurable quality improvements, and efficiencies to justify joint contracting that would otherwise trigger antitrust violations or at least concerns of the same.[8] So, while antitrust requirements have been somewhat softened, the burden is often on the CIN to prove clinical integration.

- **The Centers for Medicare & Medicaid Services (CMS) Value-Based Payment Regulations.** CINs must fall under the auspices of CMS, just like other healthcare providers and payer networks. Alternative payment models continue to be refined, and risk-based contracts and arrangements are becoming more common.[9]
- **Information Blocking Rules.** The 21st Century Cures Act provided information blocking and interoperability regulations, enforced by the Office of the National Coordinator (ONC) for Health Information Technology. The legislation requires CIN participants to ensure interoperable data sharing with limited exceptions.[10]
- **Data Privacy and Security Compliance.** Like any other healthcare operation and entity, CINs must adhere to HIPAA guidelines as well as any state-specific health privacy laws.[11]

See Chapters 13 and 15 for further discussion related to legal and regulatory issues.

AFFILIATION ROLE OF CLINICAL INTEGRATION

As noted, clinical integration and CINs specifically are a form of or an option for affiliation. They serve as a non-ownership-based affiliation model, enabling their participants, which include hospitals, physicians, and sometimes even PE groups, to jointly pursue quality and cost goals.[8] So, CINs not only have an affiliation characteristic, but they also have a practical function.

Are CINs nothing more than a bridge to value-based care? Certainly, CINs provide a platform for transitioning independent practices toward value-based contracts while preserving autonomy and independence when compared to the other forms of full affiliation.[5] Further, they allow for multi-stakeholder participation from all forms of providers, as we have mentioned previously, facilitating even greater aggregation without a legal merger of groups.

Although bound by adherence to antitrust regulations, CINs do provide a single voice. They represent myriad providers who have a common purpose that emanates from a complementary business and clinical strategy. The business of healthcare services reimbursement is vital, but the corresponding improvements in clinical care are even more valuable.

CIN affiliations serve a viable purpose as a launchpad for broader initiatives, including digital health adoption, SDoH interventions, and population health strategies.[6] AI will also be at the center of innovation.

Clinical integration is a viable affiliation option. Notwithstanding its longer-term limitations and lack of adhesiveness, it is relatively easy to create a CIN; however, many CINs are slow to realize significant financial or clinical benefit.

WRAPAROUND SERVICES AND SUPPORT

CINs are a conduit for several other services. Often, we refer to these services as wraparounds, meaning they are "wrapped around" or in addition to the core affiliation model, such as employment, or PSAs. Accordingly, these services can be included within a clinical integration agreement (CIA) that memorializes various aspects beyond just clinical integration and reimbursement initiatives alone. The following are initiatives to consider:

- **Care Management Programs**. Many CIAs offer centralized care coordination, chronic disease management, and navigation services designed to improve overall quality of care.[7]
- **Population Health Analytics**. CINs increasingly deploy advanced analytics and platforms that track outcomes, risk-stratify patients, and monitor cost-of-care trends, all in real time.[6]
- **Physician Performance Support**. For any affiliation structure, whether it's employment by a hospital, alignment with PE, or merging groups, the CIN can be an added conduit for the provision of benchmarking performance through dashboards, peer comparison reports, and targeted education. These supports help providers, especially physicians and APPs, meet quality and cost standards and targets.[8]
- **Technology Infrastructure**. Shared electronic health record (EHR) systems are at the core of clinical integration. Messaging platforms and interoperability tools enable coordinated care across the CIN.[10] These platforms and tools are by-products of CINs and, overall, promote effective affiliation among these parties.
- **SDoH Source Linkages**. Wraparound services include partnerships with community-based organizations to address patients' social needs, such as housing, food, and transportation.[7]

KEY ACCOMPLISHMENTS AND CHALLENGES

CINs are not the "end all" of affiliation models; rather, they are a supplement to the core models of employment, PSAs, etc. Serving as a wraparound is often a better scenario and a greater means of affiliation. Still, in all, there have been contracting successes with CINs, especially in a value-based multi-payer contract structure. Both upside and downside risks are often taken through CINs, improving payer alignment overall.[12]

The deliberate attention to quality and the attainment of quality metrics have led to improvement in care. Gains have been reported in preventive screening rates, chronic disease control, and reduced hospital re-admissions through such coordinated care.[8]

The effective use of care management and analytics to reduce unnecessary encounters, such as those in the emergency department, along with inpatient admissions, has been a significant positive of CINs.[7] CINs are not just for primary care providers. Specialists have learned how to expand their participation in CINs through total-cost-of-care arrangements, along with bundled payment models.[3] Notwithstanding some of these pluses, there have been challenges. It is difficult to obtain an adequate ROI from a CIN, given the capital costs of creating a CIN. Selling the CIN to demonstrate its viability and soliciting contributions toward the capital raise have stymied their growth and existence. Achieving an ROI despite infrastructure costs, limited payor participation, and uneven provider engagement has contributed to the challenges of financial sustainability.[4]

Finally, regulatory compliance creates challenges. While the focus on antitrust may be somewhat lessened now, this situation could change with shifts in the political environment and leadership.

OUTLOOK AND EMERGING TRENDS

This chapter focused on recent developments within clinical integration that increase the overall viability of the clinically integrated organization. There are more opportunities to grow and expand CINs and to realize benefits, even financial ROIs. However, there also are challenges, such as the capital needed to establish and operate CINs. In addition, their successes related to reimbursement structures are in question. More CINs are expected to transition into advanced risk-based arrangements in the future, including global budgets and capitation models, as payers push for cost accountability.[3]

The digital health integration components of CINs have been supported by specialty-focused CINs, such as oncology and orthopedics. These components are designed to optimize outcomes and costs for high-complexity patient populations.[7] CINs house such models quite well. Direct contracting might also be done through a CIN partnering with larger employers, bundled services, or comprehensive care programs outside their traditional payer channels.[5] Also, health equity metrics are an important ingredient to CIN success. Payer contracts and CINs performance dashboards increasingly include measures addressing disparities in care delivery.[7]

Finally, the future relative to regulatory changes and how they affect CINs and their operations is not only "up in the air," it can change quickly. This compliance matter has been an age-old issue. For now, CINs appear to be regulatory compliant if the entity qualifies its participants as being clinically integrated.

SUMMARY

As a form of affiliation, CINs are an option and should be considered. Do they take the place of more direct affiliation, such as employment between physicians and hospitals, or equity structures with physicians and PE-sponsored firms? Probably not. But they are a workable possibility that will continue to merit consideration.

REFERENCES

1. Federal Trade Commission withdraws health care enforcement policy standards. Federal Trade Commission Press Release. July 14, 2023. Accessed November 30, 2025. https://www.ftc.gov/news-events/news/press-releases/2023/07/federal-trade-commission-withdraws-health-care-enforcement-policy-statements.
2. Justice Department withdraws outdated enforcement policy statements. U.S. Department of Justice Press Release. February 3, 2023. Accessed August 4, 2025. https://www.justice.gov/opa/pr/justice-department-withdraws-outdated-enforcement-policy-statements.
3. Hammerstrom F. *Navigating value-based care in 2025: How to implement it successfully in your practice.* Milliman MedInsight. June 13, 2025. Accessed August 4, 2025. https://medinsight.com/healthcare-data-analytics-resources/blog/navigating-value-based-care-in-2025-how-to-implement-it-successfully-in-your-practice

4. Medical Group Management Association. *Less than half of practice leaders have positive outlook on value-based care in 2025*. MGMA Stat. February 2, 2025. Accessed August 6, 2025. https://www.mgma.com/mgma-stat/less-than-half-of-practice-leaders-positive-outlook-value-based-care-2025.
5. Marino DJ, Faber W. Evolving clinically integrated networks to prepare for value-based care in 2025. HealthITAnswers.net. Accessed August 4, 2025. https://www.healthitanswers.net/evolving-clinically-integrated-networks-to-prepare-for-value-based-care-in-2025/.
6. Lozovatsky M. Health care technology trends 2025: AI benefits, wearable use and more. American Medical Association Update. December 13, 2024. Accessed August 6, 2025. https://www.ama-assn.org/practice-management/digital-health/health-care-technology-trends-2025-ai-benefits-wearable-use-0.
7. Siegel S, Rekhraj K, Sandomirsky D, Ganhao FP, Teuber I, Fransen M. *et al.* 2025 global health care outlook. Deloitte Center for Health Solutions. January 2025. Accessed August 6, 2025. https://www.deloitte.com/us/en/insights/industry/health-care/life-sciences-and-health-care-industry-outlooks/2025-global-health-care-executive-outlook.html.
8. Clinical integration. American Hospital Association. Accessed August 4, 2025. https://www.aha.org/node/127.
9. CMS Innovation Center strategy refresh update. Centers for Medicare & Medicaid Services White Paper. January 2025. Accessed August 4, 2025. https://www.cms.gov/priorities/innovation/strategic-direction-whitepaper.
10. *Information blocking*. Office of the National Coordinator for Health Information Technology. Updated April 8, 2026. Accessed August 11, 2025. https://www.healthit.gov/topic/information-blocking.
11. Health Information privacy. U.S. Department of Health & Human Services. Accessed August 11, 2025. https://www.hhs.gov/hipaa/index.html.
12. Ohio rural hospitals form clinically integrated network. American Hospital Association Center for Health Innovation. May 6, 2025. Accessed August 11, 2025. https://www.aha.org/aha-center-health-innovation-market-scan/2025-05-06-ohio-rural-hospitals-form-clinically-integrated-network.

CHAPTER 10.

Payer Affiliation Perspective

MANY PROMINENT COMMERCIAL PAYERS, such as Kaiser Permanente, have crossed the line from being payer to provider, employing physicians and professional healthcare providers. This dynamic is not new, as large entities have been involved on both the provider and payer sides for decades. Thus, the payer side of the equation is relevant as to affiliation strategies with physicians and other providers.

The players on the payer side are a part of the broad universe of models and structures of affiliation. So, we ask and answer basic questions such as:

- Why are payers interested in being providers?
- How do they structure transactions of affiliation?
- What is the typical model?
- What is their strategic and tactical reasoning behind affiliating with providers in employment?
- What is their history? Success? Failure? Somewhere in between?
- How do they compete?

These components are important parts of the universe of affiliation strategies and call for careful review and consideration.

COMMERCIAL PAYER STRATEGIES OF AFFILIATION

In this section, we consider the prominent payers that are part of the continuum of care in the United States. Their movement toward becoming providers as well as payers has prompted careful examination of their strategies for affiliation.

Aetna (CVS Health)

Aetna has created its own accountable care/whole health collaboratives with large systems, such as Vanderbilt and Memorial Hermann. They emphasize shared data, coordinated care, and outcomes-based incentives, expanding their "Clinical Collaboration Program" for Medicare Advantage readmissions and length of stay reduction.[1,2]

The Aetna Clinical Collaboration Program's aim is to improve outcomes for its members in Medicare Advantage plans. These goals are achieved by reducing hospital readmissions and unnecessary emergency department encounters. The program places nurses on-site to assist hospital staff with care decisions. The nurses support the patients upon discharge and often shift them to skilled nursing facilities or their home healthcare.[3]

The parent company, CVS, employs some providers. For example, the company owns Oak Street Health, which is a value-based senior primary care clinic facility. They also own Signify Health, which conducts in-home evaluations and care coordination programs. This creates a vertical pathway for Aetna members without Aetna itself employing most physicians.[4]

Programs that have worked for Aetna include early accountable-care products that reported lower costs and better coordination in multiple markets. Risk and quality management have been effectively implemented.[1] In 2024, Signify Health experienced a record year of home health evaluations (over three million), including nearly doubling the number of Aetna members served.[5] These affiliation models have stopped short of full employment.

As to the future of such programs, Aetna is expected to continue steering Medicare Advantage and accountable care members into Oak Street clinics and in-home care. More hospital "clinical collaboration" deals will be considered in efforts to limit readmissions and excess hospital stays.

From all indications, Aetna and these programs of affiliation have experienced strong top-line growth. However, it is reported that medical costs continue to rise and function as a strong headwind toward growing these models with greater success.[6]

United Healthcare (Optum)

United Healthcare has been aggressive in its physician affiliation strategies in that they have completed large-scale employment and/or contracting transactions through Optum. These include medical groups, ambulatory surgical centers, home health, etc. Optum has also been active in putting together extensive value-based arrangements. They had served approximately 4.7 million people in value-based care by the end of 2024.[7]

Optum is, in fact, the largest employer of physicians in the United States, with a network of about 90,000 physicians who are employed, contracted, or otherwise affiliated.[8] Optum has assembled a broad care platform. For example, DaVita Medical Group, LHC Group, and Change Healthcare align the delivery and provision of services with payer contracting.[9]

Optum has experienced significant financial growth and has spent millions in capital investment in its affiliation strategies development. Vertical integration conflicts have resulted, but overall, Optum has been successful, largely attributable to data-driven, value-based initiatives.[7] They provide significant practice support and financial stability.

It is reported that some specialists have been less than pleased about below-market compensation and bonus structures. In comparison to primary care providers, the specialist's attrition is greater.[10] Nonetheless, as Optum's influence in the marketplace relative to affiliation transactions grows, some physicians report losing clinical autonomy and decision-making power. For some, the expected, and to some extent promised, "independence" shifts to corporate control over key aspects of their practice.[10]

As to the future, Optum/United should continue with physician-related healthcare provider roll-ups and look toward specific areas of reimbursement, to include taking on more risk via capitation. Regulatory and antitrust friction could shape the future within this multi-billion-dollar organization.[11]

Cigna (The Cigna Group/Evernorth)

Cigna has experienced limited direct employment through its Evernorth Care Group (formerly Cigna Medical Group). These are multispecialty clinics with broader alignment now through Evernorth management and oversight.[12] Cigna seeks extensive collaboration with hospitals and health systems through provider enablement to improve care quality, control costs, and enhance patient experience. They are using their Care Allies unit to support quality metrics, data sharing, care coordination, and value-based contracting.

Their strategy and initiatives have been successful and somewhat "under the radar," drawing fewer headlines in relation to physician acquisitions and related transactions. They have thus had less exposure and risk of antitrust pressures.[13] The Cigna Value-Based Partnerships that have formed have experienced some success and strengthened care delivery, cost savings, and patient outcomes.[13]

Regarding the future, incremental clinic growth is expected, especially within existing markets with more virtual/specialty enablement. Cigna's model entails more contractual relationships with providers rather than mass employment.[14]

Blue Cross Blue Shield (the Blues Plans)[15]

Blue Cross Blue Shield (BCBS) plans generally do not involve employment of physicians to any significant degree. Instead, most Blue Cross Blue Shield state plans lead in value-based contracts with shared savings and risk engaging with non-affiliated practices and hospitals. Examples include:

- **BCBS Massachusetts** – An alternative quality contract (AQC) exists, wherein global budgets tied to quality incentives across large groups are applied.[16]
- **Blue Cross North Carolina** – The Blue Premier program is statewide, entailing joint accountability with hospitals and physicians. Recently, it was reported that $801 million cumulative savings have been realized since 2019.[17]
- **BCBS Michigan** – This state has formulated a Physician Group Incentive Program (PGIP), resulting in patient-centered medical homes and incentive dollars tied to quality and spending controls.[18]

Peer-reviewed evidence shows quality improvements and spending moderation under budget-plus quality models implemented within the various states by their BCBS entity. The results have varied by market and require data infrastructure and strong provider partners.[19] BCBC data and analytics initiatives have included partnerships that emphasize data sharing, real-time analytics, and health information exchanges to enhance care coordination, risk management, chronic condition management, and reduce overall emergency room utilization.[20]

Humana

Humana has a significant employment/ownership footprint via its Center Well/Conviva senior primary care clinics and home health. At the end of 2024, 340 centers existed, serving over 390,000 seniors. The clinics are rapidly expanding, including a presence in Walmart locations.[21] An employment model exists in that Humana owns CenterWell, a value-based senior primary care clinic entity. Also, Conviva (Senior Care) creates a vertical pathway for Humana members without Humana itself employing most providers, giving expanded access to primary care.

As for success, Humana has realized scale in senior primary care, wherein it has partnered with Medicare Advantage risk performance. Their execution of risk includes clinic ramp economics and market selection.[22] They have negotiated reimbursement rates that stay competitive, promoting value-based arrangements that reward providers for efficiency, quality, and outcome achievement, rather than volume. The patient experience prioritizes providers with admitting privileges at network hospitals, ensuring continuity of care and patient satisfaction.

Humana has filed lawsuits against the Centers for Medicare & Medicaid Services (CMS) over downgraded ratings, citing errors in how the scores were calculated. The resulting regulatory uncertainty affects the stability and effectiveness of these partnering programs.[23]

As for the future, expect more such clinics, independent physician association (IPA)-type expansion, including CINs, and embedded specialty home health services.[4] These will be shifting to value-based care with emphasis on quality and more efficient care coordination efforts.

Kaiser Permanente

Kaiser Permanente is an integrated "staff-/group-model" system that combines a health plan (Kaiser Foundation Health Plan), hospital/facility arm (Kaiser Foundation Hospitals), and regionally governed, physician-led Permanente Medical Groups. It operates a prepaid (capitated) model in which most care for members is delivered by Permanente physicians in KP facilities, aligning financing and delivery under one umbrella. Founded in 1945, KP now serves approximately 12.6–13.1 million members across limited U.S. regions.[24,25]

Historically, KP grows through de-novo facilities and membership in its regions rather than broad national contracting. In 2023–2024, it created Risant Health, a KP-affiliated nonprofit platform to bring KP's value-based playbook to community health systems; the first acquisition (Geisinger) closed March 31, 2024, with KP signaling intent to add more systems. This extends KP's affiliation footprint beyond classic KP HMO regions while keeping acquired systems non-KP-branded.[26]

Value-based reimbursement is native to KP's architecture: Members pay a prepaid premium, and Permanente groups are funded to manage total cost and outcomes — essentially global budgets with internal incentives tied to quality, access, and equity. KP's own policy outlets and physician federation describe a comprehensive value model (care integration, data/IT, care pathways, prevention, and population health management). In Medicare Advantage, KP consistently earns high Star Ratings (4.0–4.5 stars across regions).[27,28]

Relative to the broader market, several aspects are working well. For example, tight plan-provider alignment and physician-led governance support standardized, team-based care and evidence-based pathways. KP's Medicare Advantage contracts continue to post high CMS Star Ratings in multiple markets for 2025–2026, reflecting strong chronic care management and patient experience versus many peers.[27] The Risant platform is a notable strategy innovation — exporting KP's value-based capabilities to non-KP systems (starting with Geisinger) without forcing full KP integration, potentially widening KP's influence in national value-based care diffusion.[26]

Constraints and challenges include access and network breadth, in that KP's "closed" network model can limit choice; national analyses of narrow networks highlight trade-offs that KP's HMO design exemplifies (choice vs. coordination/cost). California regulators and media have cited persistent deficiencies in KP mental health access and grievance handling, including significant fines and ongoing scrutiny,[29] and repeated labor disputes and planned/actual strikes underscore staffing pressures that can affect access and operations.[30] Also, despite its size, KP's fully integrated model remains concentrated in specific regions; national scaling requires new vehicles (e.g., Risant) rather than traditional payer contracting.

For independent physician groups, KP affiliation typically means employment within a Permanente Medical Group or practice within KP facilities — far closer integration than standard payer contracts. Outside KP regions, the Risant path suggests partnerships with community systems that keep local brands but adopt KP's value infrastructure (care redesign, analytics, risk management). This creates a third affiliation archetype in many markets: (1) payer-provider "virtual" VBR, (2) health-system employment, and now (3) KP-style integrated/risk platform affiliation via Risant.

Kaiser Permanente's staff-/group-model and prepaid financing make it the U.S. archetype for value-based integration. Performance signals (quality and MA stars) remain strong; the major challenges are access constraints, behavioral health compliance, and workforce stability. The Risant strategy is KP's vehicle to influence VBR beyond its legacy footprint — worth tracking as it adds additional systems and proves (or fails to prove) portability at scale.

SUMMARY

This brief glimpse of affiliation strategies among the payers creates yet another level of alternatives for physicians and other providers to consider. Prominent payers have equipped the market with significant financial and management capital, much of which is dedicated to some form of value-based reimbursement. Thus, one could conclude that the payers have indeed been active in implementing specific and direct strategies with providers, and these largely entail reimbursement that is more value-based as opposed to volume-based.

As a result, we expect continued emphasis on these areas. For example, the Blues emphasize contractual value-based care with peer review results. Humana stresses employment with a risk of managing total cost. Large payer providers, however, will face continued increased media and antitrust attention, which may slow or reshape their affiliation transactional activity. Finally, we emphasize that many states have corporate practice of medicine limitations relative to direct insurer employment of providers. These threats have pushed the providers, such as the Blues, toward more contractual relationships than ownership and employment.

Therefore, payers as providers are not a small part of the healthcare affiliation strategies paradigm. Payers, like those considered above, have significant involvement in physician and other provider affiliation initiatives. In fact, with the general populace being somewhat unaware of their involvement, it will be interesting as the future unfolds for more exposure from both the media and government vis-à-vis antitrust relative to these prominent payers' involvement with physicians, *et. al.*

As a result, payer-provider relationships will likely continue to grow, with providers taking the lead in value-based reimbursement initiatives as they employ and contract with physicians, along with hospitals and health systems.

REFERENCES

1. Ayers W. New Aetna accountable care product leverages strengths of Vanderbilt Health Affiliated Network. VUMC News. September 19, 2017. Accessed November 30, 2025. https://news.vumc.org/2017/09/19/new-aetna-accountable-care-product-leverages-strengths-of-vanderbilt-health-affiliated-network/.
2. The Aetna and Memorial Hermann Accountable Care Network. Memorial Hermann. Accessed September 22, 2025. https://memorialhermann.org/about-us/our-organization/aco/aetna-accountable-care-network.
3. CVS Health. Aetna expands clinical collaboration program to enhance support for hospitals and provide personalized member care. CVS Health. September 22, 2025. Accessed November 30, 2025. https://www.cvshealth.com/news/company-news/aetna-expands-clinical-collaboration-program.html.
4. Meyersohn N. CVS buys Oak Street Health in $10.6 billion deal. CNN Business. February 9, 2023. Accessed November 30, 2025. https://www.cnn.com/2023/02/09/business/cvs-oak-street-health#:~:text=New%20York%20CNN%20%E2%80%94,to%20move%20into%20the%20area.
5. CVS Health 2024 annual review. CVS Health. Accessed November 30, 2025. https://cvshealth2024inreview.com.
6. Mondal M. CVS health care delivery: will the growth momentum last in Q2? Yahoo Finance. July 30, 2025. Accessed November 30, 2025. https://finance.yahoo.com/news/cvs-health-care-delivery-growth-122300185.html.
7. UnitedHealth Group reports 2024 results. UnitedHealth Group Press Release. January 16, 2025. Accessed November 30, 2025. https://www.unitedhealthgroup.com/content/dam/UHG/PDF/investors/2024/2025-16-01-uhg-reports-fourth-quarter-results.pdf.
8. Herman B, Bannow T, Ross C, Lawrenc, L. How UnitedHealth harnesses its physician empire to squeeze profits out of patients. PNHP. July 25, 2024. Accessed September 25, 2025. https://pnhp.org/news/how-unitedhealth-harnesses-its-physician-empire-to-squeeze-profits-out-of-patients/.
9. Newitt P. Optum's quiet physician empire in 24 numbers. Becker's ASC. July 31, 2025. Accessed November 30, 2025. https://www.beckersasc.com/asc-transactions-and-valuation-issues/optums-quiet-physician-empire-in-24-numbers/.
10. Lawrence L, Ross C, Herman B, Bannow T. UnitedHealth pledged a hands-off approach after buying a Connecticut medical group. Then it upended how doctors practice. STAT News. August 28, 2024. Accessed November 30, 2025. https://www.statnews.com/2024/08/28/unitedhealth-optum-prohealth-physicians-care-squeezed-for-profit-doctors-say/.
11. Form 10-K, fiscal year ended December 31, 2024. UnitedHealth Group. 2025. Accessed November 30, 2025. https://www.unitedhealthgroup.com/content/dam/UHG/PDF/investors/2024/UNH-Q4-2024-Form-10-K.pdf.

12. Cigna medical group to expand health services to more people, changes name to Evernorth Care Group. Evernorth Press Release. August 30, 2022. Accessed November 30, 2025. https://www.evernorth.com/cigna-medical-group-to-expand-and-changes-name-to-evernorth-care-group.
13. Annual report (Form 10-K) for year ended February 29, 2024. Cigna Group. 2024. Accessed November 30, 2025. https://fintel.io/doc/sec-cigna-group-1739940-10k-2024-february-29-19782-9537.
14. Evernorth Health Services. The Cigna Group. Accessed September 22, 2025. https://www.thecignagroup.com/our-capabilities/evernorth-health-services
15. Blue Cross Blue Shield plans are independent and vary significantly by state. Thus, our discussion is limited on a very high-level overall basis.
16. Blue Cross Blue Shield of Massachusetts. The alternative quality contract. KFF. May 2010. Accessed November 30, 2025. https://www.kff.org/wp-content/uploads/sites/2/2012/07/alternative-quality-contract.pdf.
17. Blue Cross and Blue Shield of North Carolina. (2025, March 19). *Blue Premier 2023 results: driving quality and cost savings.* Blue Cross NC. March 19, 2025. https://www.bluecrossnc.com/providers/provider-news/2025/blue-premier-2023-results-driving-quality-cost-savings.
18. Value partnerships. Blue Cross Blue Shield Blue Care Network of Michigan. Accessed September 22, 2025. https://www.bcbsm.com/providers/network/value-partnerships/.
19. McWilliams J, Landon BE, Chernow ME. Changes in health care spending and quality for Medicare beneficiaries associated with a commercial ACO contract. *JAMA*; 310(8): 829–836. Accessed November 30, 2024. https://doi.org/10.1001/jama.2013.276302.
20. Blue Cross and Blue Shield of Georgia and Emory Healthcare announce partnership to improve health care delivery model. Emory News. January 22, 2014. Accessed November 30, 2025. https://news.emory.edu/stories/2014/01/ehc_bcbs_partnership/.
21. CenterWell poised for further primary care expansion in 2025. Humana Press Release. February 19, 2025. Accessed November 30, 2025. https://policy.humana.com/issue-area/news-and-resources/news-press/2025/centerwell-poised-for-further-primary-care-expansion-in.
22. Pifer R. Humana plans to add up to 30 more primary care centers this year. Healthcare Dive. February 19, 2025. Accessed November 30, 2025. https://www.healthcaredive.com/news/humana-centerwell-conviva-primary-care-2025-expansion/740347.
23. Pifer R. Judge dismisses Humana's Medicare Advantage star ratings suit. Healthcare Dive. July 18, 2025. Accessed November 30, 2025. https://www.healthcaredive.com/news/humana-medicare-advantage-star-ratings-lawsuit-dismissed/753455/.

24. Our model: Integrated care and coverage. Kaiser Permanente. Accessed November 30, 2025. https://about.kaiserpermanente.org/expertise-and-impact/public-policy/integrated-care.
25. Our care model. Permanente Medicine. June 11, 2025. Accessed November 30, 2025. https://permanente.org/about-us/our-care-model/.
26. Muoio D. Kaiser Permanente's Risant Health completes Geisinger Health acquisition. Fierce Healthcare. April 2, 2024. Accessed November 30, 2025. https://www.fiercehealthcare.com/providers/kaiser-permanentes-risant-health-completes-geisinger-health-acquisition.
27. 2025 Medicare Star Ratings: Kaiser Permanente health plans highly rated by CMS. Kaiser Permanente. October 14, 2024. Accessed November 30, 2025. https://about.kaiserpermanente.org/news/press-release-archive/2025-medicare-star-ratings-kaiser-permanente-health-plans-highly-rated-by-cms.
28. Unlocking the potential of value-based care. Permanente Medicine. Accessed November 30, 2025. https://permanente.org/medical-excellence/unlocking-the-potential-of-value-based-care/.
29. Wolfson BJ. Kaiser Permanente back in the hot seat over mental health care, but it's not only a KP issue. California Healthline. February 6, 2025. Accessed November 30, 2025. https://californiahealthline.org/news/article/kaiser-permanente-mental-health-parity.
30. Weiss H. What's at stake with the Kaiser Permanente health care strike. *TIME*. October 4, 2023. Accessed November 30, 2025. https://time.com/6320607/kaiser-permanente-heath-care-strike-whats-at-stake.

CHAPTER 11.
The Role of Advisers

When medical groups and healthcare providers consider affiliation, regardless of the option, the underlying question centers on whether to procure outside assistance to facilitate the process.

The role of an adviser must be balanced with the value that the adviser provides. Advisers are not cheap, but advisers who can create added value and complete a more desirable transaction because of their experience, expertise, and overall skill will pay for themselves.

Thousands, if not millions of dollars, may be at stake, depending on the decision about who will provide this assistance (either from the sell- or buy-side consultation). Thus, the value proposition and the role of advisers should be considered carefully, and a decision made prior to engaging extensively with the prospective affiliation partner. Initial steps include engaging the adviser, negotiating the fees, and accepting that this cost is necessary.

VALUE PROPOSITION

Fundamentally, the entity that is seeking advisory assistance (either the buying or selling side) should first identify the reasons for hiring an adviser and solidify the overall expectations or value propositions. The adviser should provide accretive value, meaning that by their mere involvement, they decrease the client's stress and help them realize a net improved economic (and non-economic to some extent) result.

The financial and related terms of the adviser's work should be documented explicitly and considered prior to agreement. These terms are memorialized within the engagement agreement and should be a significant part of the overall decision.

A good adviser also serves as a "buffer" or go-between on behalf of the client. The actual transaction itself will flow better because of this "go-between" expertise.

Another benefit of having an experienced adviser is their ability to evaluate not only the affiliation alternatives, but also the specific variables from one offer to another.

Another way for advisers to establish their value is by having a sixth sense of who best fits with their client. After getting to know the client, understanding their nuances and overt and covert expectations, the ideal adviser should be able to recognize and evaluate whether the parties are a proper fit and have common cultures. Being confident that they will do their due diligence on behalf of the client to understand its makeup, from the personalities to its historical performance, is important.

The ability to evaluate offers and determine how they compare with one another, ranging from the indication of interest (IOI), letter of intent (LOI), and definitive agreements, is a special skill to consider when selecting an adviser. Good advisers understand their client's individual as well as collective markets, as well as the entire industry, and know how best the client will fit within the market structure. This is a special, yet nebulous, skill set that can pay huge dividends to the client.

Engaging an adviser who can bring a full package of expertise, including financial analyses and other related services, to provide a "virtual one-stop shop" is preferable to piecemealing the assignments for assistance. Also, the ability to consolidate expertise and subsequent services to the client often results in a net lower cost.

The final prerequisite for selecting an adviser is their ability to negotiate the difficult issues that inevitably exist within each potential transaction, consolidate the challenges, and recognize when a deal is possible with a particular organization and when it should be abandoned. With this expertise, the adviser will save the client considerable time and money.

COST AND FEE OPTIONS

Cost and fee structures for advisers vary. The most common arrangement is a combination of fixed fees, such as a retainer, especially at the beginning of a working relationship, to be applied toward an incentive fee based on the performance and the completion of a transaction. The fees depend on the transaction's size and the required assistance.

If, for example, a medical group has already done a great deal of legwork and identified one or even two or three possible affiliation partners, the work of the adviser may be limited. Conversely, if the adviser begins to collaborate with the client from the outset with multiple acquirers/partners, much more work is required to sort out and eliminate those who are not viable. This adds up to potentially a greater total value of the transaction, but also requires more work from the adviser. Consequently, the fees will be higher.

The fees should be tied to the size of the transaction. In many PE transactions where an income scrape has resulted, deriving an earnings before interest, taxes, depreciation, and amortization (EBITDA) total to then be applied with a market-based multiple to result in total enterprise value, that prospective amount is the basis for the adviser fees.

For example, let's say we have a restated EBITDA of $5 million per year for the group. A market-based multiple of 10 would render a value of $50 million. That $50 million enterprise value, if procured, would cover all facets of the transaction for the seller whom the adviser is representing. Even the rollover of say 20% or $10 million resulting in a $40 million payout would be a part of the total transaction value and, thus, the basis on which the adviser's fee would be assigned. That fee, based on a $50 million enterprise value, could encompass retention and/or any fixed portion of the fee, though given the situation, those fees may be in addition to the performance fee.

Indeed, the percentage may vary not only based on the amount that is fixed, but also on the amount applied, whether directly or indirectly, against the percentage fee. It may be tiered based on the adviser's ability to negotiate and realize the best possible total enterprise value.

In the example above, a $50 million deal with $40 million paid at closing could be structured where the first $30 million of that transaction is at an agreed-upon percentage, say 2.5%. Any additional value obtained above $30 million could be paid at a smaller percentage, such as 2%, with the final $10 million rollover amount paid at 1%.

These are examples and should not be considered standard. They simply show the way the process works. The more enterprise value realized by the adviser on behalf of their client, the greater the total performance fee, even though the percentages might be less as the value increases. The overall fee in such an example is obviously quite a lot, but the adviser may well work for months to identify a list of potential buyers, and home in on the one or two finalists, and then ultimately the final one to complete the transaction. Thus, the adviser has earned their extra layer of costs by the mere fact that they have created maximum enterprise value.

Other concepts within the fee structure include fixed retainers over an initial period of months for the adviser to invest time and effort toward understanding and learning more about the client to represent them best and start the process of developing teasers and other information. Additionally, the adviser will review historical financials, even completing the Quality of Earnings (QofE).

All these factors can be subject to retainers and/or fixed fees. They may be assigned on a fee-for-service (FFS) basis, based on a rate per hour of time completed for such initial services. Earnouts may be applied, meaning that if the adviser procures a higher total enterprise value, that differential is paid at that time. If the client obtains payment for its value after closing via an earnout, the adviser may get a percentage of that earnout as realized at that time.

Finally, most advisers will agree to have a significant amount of their fees tied to at-risk structures. In other words, they only earn the "big bucks" when that additional enterprise value is realized. Varying percentages may apply, but even at a lower percentage (as illustrated above), the incentive exists to maximize value and thus earn a higher total incentive fee.

Expenses should also be reimbursed, including the cost of travel and other out-of-pocket items, along with advertising attributable to the sale or other transactional terms.

As for total fee structures paid to an adviser, it is safe to say that every deal should be negotiated as to fee structure based on its own merits, size of the transaction, and other items of the value proposition. While it is typical to combine fixed or retainer fees with performance-based fees, every deal should be structured based on its individual qualities and the ability of the adviser to achieve the results desired by the client. Sometimes, the more difficult the transaction is, the higher the payment. In other words, the adviser receives a "bonus" for completing a challenging transaction that is recognized by all on the front side of the engagement.

What if the transaction fails to take place? What fee does the client pay to the adviser? This is negotiable, but usually under a performance-based fee structure, the adviser gets only the portion of their fees that were recognized and agreed upon as definitive, regardless of whether a transaction closes. Often, advisers will want to evaluate the situation and incorporate some additional fees when it is understood that a transaction is not necessarily guaranteed. Again, everything is negotiable.

Finally, the client looking to hire the adviser should consider more than a single adviser, creating a market with competition for the fee structure, plus the services and the expertise supporting the same. This situation is not only common, but it should also be done in every case.

BUY-SIDE VERSUS SELL-SIDE ADVISER ROLES

Seeking and engaging professional advisers for PE and/or other external transactions involves similarities and variances. The buy-side adviser helps the potential purchaser within the transaction and, as such, provides a universe of viable legal entities to consider. The engagement is usually structured with the adviser retained and paid a guaranteed fixed amount per month until the actual entity to purchase is identified. The entire transaction could be at risk for the adviser, especially if there are myriad potential entities to acquire. Usually, the adviser will also complete some due diligence to prepare the potential purchaser to consider those entities within the overall acquisition.

Once a PE firm has acquired a business and established a defined platform, the development experts within that advisory firm, or even within the platform being formed, provide the buy-side analysis. This analysis includes some basic discussions about the merits of the entity under consideration.

From a buy-side perspective, the identification of potential acquisitions, particularly within an existing platform, should initially entail consideration of a wide variety of companies. The buy-side adviser should quickly analyze these entities, and if there is sufficient interest and the performance history warrants (e.g., meets the criteria established for acquisitions, such as prior historical performance, EBITDA status, etc.), the pursuit of acquisition is underway.

If the development team for the platform (often a PE-oriented platform) is an in-house adviser, the compensation for the buy-side work may be inherent to their employment and related compensation, along with some incentives for deal closures. These incentives could be a percentage of the total deal or some other metric established alongside the employment compensation amounts.

Sell-side representation takes on a different role, as this is usually an outside party that is the expert to support the sell-side advisory services. The associated fees are consistent with those outlined earlier. The sell-side advisory will also conduct a fair amount of due diligence and possibly some reverse due diligence management. The sell-side advisory is interested in completing a transaction, especially once a specific buyer entity is identified. Much time and effort are usually spent completing all the processes, including the definitive negotiations, collaborating with legal counsel, and the buy-side adviser, as well.

Therefore, the role of both sell-side and buy-side advisers is to initially identify prospects, evaluate their viability, and determine whether they are an initial fit. If so, the adviser works through the entire process for the transaction's completion. They justify their participation (and their fees) through their independence and detailed functionality, culminating in negotiation expertise. If these things occur, a transaction is likely.

BROKER-DEALER CREDENTIALS

As PE transactions become more prominent along with other merger and acquisition scenarios, the question is warranted of whether a sell- or buy-side adviser should be registered with applicable governmental oversight agencies. Many advisers who provide merger and acquisition (M&A) consulting services to hospitals and health systems, PE-backed firms, and other investors within the healthcare arena must consider this situation carefully. Advisers who provide a variety of M&A advice and guidance are subject to such licensing.

Generally, if these transactions do not involve the purchase or sale of securities, registration as a broker-dealer with the U.S. Securities and Exchange Commission (SEC), and/or the Financial Industry Regulatory Authority (FINRA), or any specific state agency is not required. Nonetheless, diligent assessment must be given on this matter with each M&A transaction under review. A firm that provides M&A services in connection with transactions that involve the purchase or sale of securities would require a higher level of certification and approval from governmental agencies such as the SEC or FINRA. Any advisory firm may provide those services if it complies with the requirements for an M&A broker under the Securities Exchange Act of 1934.[1]

While advisory services firms may not be required to be a registered broker-dealer, this criterion may change over time. For example, in the future, certain transactions may involve the purchase or sale of securities, whereas previously this was not the case. Also, as laws change, the adviser should remain fully apprised of these boundaries.

The following paragraphs consider the requirements for broker-dealers to register with those governmental agencies. Requirements vary by state, and each adviser should consider the parameters for revisions within the states in which they provide M&A services.

THE GENERAL REQUIREMENT FOR BROKER-DEALERS TO REGISTER

Under the Exchange Act, a "broker" is "any person engaged in the business of effecting transactions in securities for the account of others" [15 U.S.C. § 78c(a)(4)(A)]. A "dealer" is "any person engaged in the business of buying and selling securities ... for such person's own account through a broker or otherwise" [15 U.S.C. § 78c(a)(5)(A)]. And a "security" is defined broadly to include "any note, stock, ... bond, debenture, ... transferable share, [or] investment contract," among other instruments [15 U.S.C. § 78c(a)(10)].

In determining whether a person or entity acts as a broker, the SEC considers several questions, including: (1) whether they participate in important parts of a securities transaction such as solicitation, negotiation, or execution; (2) whether their compensation for the transaction depends on the outcome or size of the transaction; (3) whether they are otherwise engaged in the business of effecting or facilitating securities transactions; and (4) whether they handle the securities or funds of others in connection with securities transactions.[2]

According to the SEC, a "yes" answer to any of these questions may indicate broker activity. Additionally, the SEC has advised that a broker's activities may include, among other things, "[f]inding buyers and sellers of businesses (i.e., activities relating to mergers and acquisitions where securities are involved)." Again, the key threshold of requiring broker/dealer registration is whether the purchase or sale of securities is involved.

If a person or entity falls within the definition of a broker or dealer, they must register with the SEC. The Exchange Act makes it "unlawful" for any broker-dealer "to make use of the mails or any means or instrumentality of interstate commerce to effect any transactions in, or to induce or attempt to induce the purchase or sale of, any security ... unless such broker or dealer is registered" [15 U.S.C. § 78o(a)(1)].

Generally, the broker-dealer registration process entails: (1) filing a Form BD with the SEC and having the SEC approve the registration; (2) becoming a member of a self-regulatory organization such as FINRA; (3) becoming a member of the Securities Investor Protection Corporation ("SIPC"); (4) complying with all applicable state law requirements; and (5) the broker-dealer's associated persons must satisfy applicable qualification requirements.[2]

Conducting broker-dealer activities without registration exposes a firm or individual to potential enforcement action by the SEC or FINRA that may include remedies such as injunctions, disgorgement, civil money penalties, and industry bars — not to mention reputational damage and legal fees. [See, for example, In re McCabe, Exchange Act Release No. 102230 (Jan. 17, 2025) (ordering remedies including civil penalties and permanent industry bar based on unregistered broker activity); In re Shabat, Exchange Act Release No. 102174 (Jan. 14, 2025) (ordering remedies including disgorgement with prejudgment interest, civil penalties, and six-month industry bar based on unregistered broker activity); SEC v. GEL Direct Trust, Litigation Release No. 26092 (Aug. 30, 2024) (describing final judgments in district court action, which included injunctions and civil penalties, based on unregistered broker activities). Absent proper certification and meeting registration exemption (see below), the penalties are significant.

THE REGISTRATION EXEMPTION FOR M&A BROKERS

The Exchange Act has an exemption from registration for an "M&A broker" [15 U.S.C. § 78o(b)(13)(A)]. But the M&A broker exemption is quite limited, as described below.

An M&A broker means a broker "engaged in the business of effecting securities transactions solely in connection with the transfer of ownership of an eligible privately held company," if the broker reasonably believes that (1) upon consummation of the transaction, the person acquiring securities or assets of the eligible privately held company will control that company and be active in its management, and, (2) prior to becoming legally bound, the person will receive the most recent fiscal financial statements of the issuer of the securities [15 U.S.C. § 78o(b)(13)(E)(iv)].

The Exchange Act defines an "eligible privately held company" as a company that (1) does not have any class of securities registered, or required to be registered, with the SEC, and (2) in the fiscal year before the M&A broker was engaged for the securities transaction had (a) earnings before interest, taxes, depreciation, and amortization of less than $25 million or (b) gross revenues of less than $250 million [15 U.S.C. § 78o(b)(13)(E)(iii)].

Further limiting the availability of the M&A exemption, the Exchange Act provides that an M&A broker "is not exempt from registration" if they engage in any of the following activities:

(1) in connection with the transfer of ownership of an eligible privately held company, receiving, holding, transmitting, or having custody of funds or securities to be exchanged;
(2) participating in a public offering of registered securities;
(3) engaging in a transaction involving a shell company except in certain situations;
(4) providing financing related to the transfer of ownership of an eligible privately held company;
(5) assisting a party to obtain financing from a third party without complying with applicable laws and disclosing any compensation in writing;
(6) representing both the buyer and seller in the same transaction without written disclosure as to whom the broker represents and written consent from both parties;
(7) facilitating a transaction with a group of buyers formed with assistance from the M&A broker to acquire an eligible privately held company;
(8) engaging in a transaction involving the transfer of ownership of an eligible privately held company to a passive buyer or group of passive buyers; or
(9) binding a party to a transfer of ownership of an eligible privately held company" [15 U.S.C. § 78o(b)(13)(B)].

Thus, qualifying for the M&A exemption is limited and should be reviewed carefully. If doubts about qualifying for the exemption exist, the adviser should seek legal counsel to ascertain its status.

BROKER–DEALER CONCLUSIONS

In conclusion, each situation should be considered on its merits, and if there is any possibility of a transaction involving a purchase or sale of securities, the adviser must make this known prior to being engaged. Providing services of a buy- or sell-side nature, as discussed in this chapter, is not required if they relate to transactions that do not involve the purchase or sale of securities. If, however, a firm starts to or is ever asked to deliver the same advisory services as currently existent, but the transaction involves the purchase or sale of securities, they may be within the definition of a broker under the Exchange Act.

The SEC has documented that broker activity may include finding buyers and sellers of businesses and activities related to M&A where securities are involved, as these are typical credentials of such advisory firms. Moreover, if the adviser wants to provide M&A services in connection with transactions involving securities without registering, such may be possible via the M&A broker exemption. That exemption requires (1) the relevant transactions involve "eligible privately held companies," as described in 15 U.S.C. § 78o(b)(13)(A), and (2) the firm does not engage in any of the nine activities that would negate the exemption. Overall, a continual review should be completed to ensure that either the exemption applies or there is no purchase or sale of securities within the M&A transaction.

When an advisory firm is under consideration for engagement, the prospective client of that firm should ascertain its broker-dealer status, especially if their transaction involves the purchase or sale of securities. If not, the potential advisory firm should meet all other qualifications as identified in this chapter.

LEGAL COUNSEL ROLES AND DUTIES

One of the most important components of completing any transaction of affiliation is competent legal counsel. Like the characteristics of buy- and sell-side advisers, legal counsel should be thoroughly experienced in having completed such transactions. Moreover, legal counsel should understand the details and the regulatory and compliance standards that healthcare-related entities must consistently adhere to. Attorneys with such expertise represent both sides within any affiliation transaction.

For hospital deals, often the expert legal counsel is in-house, with some utilization of outside firms, depending upon the transaction's complexity. Hospitals have specific regulatory boundaries they must meet. Thus, legal counsel for both the buyer and the seller of any hospital transaction must be thoroughly experienced and knowledgeable in Stark and anti-kickback statutes, antitrust, and other relevant legal matters.

The sell-side adviser should be equally knowledgeable, as sometimes practices overlook this vital component; that is, having competent healthcare legal counsel assisting them throughout the sell-side process, whether it is with hospitals, PE, or some other outside party as the acquirer.

Legal costs are a part of the entire continuum of completing the transaction. These costs can be high, and to the extent the seller can utilize the buyer's (or, in some cases, the hospital's) legal expertise to mitigate their costs, this should be worthy of consideration. Saving legal fees can be a mistake, however. Without the utilization of proper legal representation, mistakes or even poorly structured transactions that improperly favor the buyer may occur. Being "pennywise and pound-foolish" when it comes to legal costs and expertise utilization should not occur, even though the costs seem quite high and difficult to justify.

TAX ADVISERS

Income tax and other related taxes are important considerations within any affiliation transaction. Both buyers and sellers must consider their effect. This should be the case even under a not-for-profit health system that is acquiring a medical practice.

Good tax advice is worth the cost and should be a part of the "checklist" of things covered and considered prior to closing the transaction. Waiting to get good advice, especially for the for-profit entities, is a huge mistake if they wait until after the transaction is near completion or completed. These matters must be carefully considered within the overall process of finalizing an affiliation transaction.

Often, physician groups neglect (or overlook) the importance of considering the tax ramifications of whatever deal they are structuring. For example, most transactions with medical practices and hospitals (and in many cases PE) are asset purchases. This is opposed to the legal entity itself being acquired. From a tax standpoint, there are various pros and cons to structuring asset versus entity acquisitions. Usually, the former is the preferred way. Being able to obtain capital gains rates, which are much lower than ordinary income rates, on any gain that a sale entails to that selling entity, such as the medical practice, is extremely important. It could result in the deal being completed, depending on the income tax ramifications. Therefore, these features are all important, not to be overlooked within the overall purview of advisory services.

POST-TRANSACTION INTEGRATION

While we are focused on the transaction itself and completing it with adequate and qualified advisory expertise, it is essential to think through the post-transaction needs and the continuum of advisory services that are necessary. Once an acquisition is finalized, the integration of that entity into the acquiring platform is a major challenge and subject to more mistakes. Negative outcomes could be financially devastating to meeting the goals and objectives, financial and otherwise, of the deal. Therefore, having a strong integration/implementation plan, post-transaction, and utilizing outside experts, as appropriate, is essential to the overall continuum of these transactions.

Waiting until after the deal closes to determine the integration steps, processes, and responsibilities of who is leading these functions can be a disastrous mistake. The postponement could result in the entire transaction getting off on the wrong foot and/or being economically devastating. Therefore, determining who will do the integration and whether this will be an outside expert if done internally is an essential part of the decision-making centered around the role of advisers.

FREQUENTLY ASKED QUESTIONS

As we consider the points discussed above, there are inevitably questions that arise and should be asked and answered prior to either the buyer or the seller deciding to utilize advisory assistance, and then to decide who would be the best adviser. Following is a list of common questions and brief responses to each one.

1. Considering their costs, do advisers earn their fees?
This answer is obviously subjective and varied. Skilled, experienced, and knowledgeable healthcare advisers, whether sell-side or buy-side, do earn their fees by the accretive results they help to achieve. While costly, specific services and value usually can be concluded after the fact, and thus, the skilled and experienced advisers have completed their task thoroughly and confidently. Some level of assessment and accountability should be established throughout the process that periodically evaluates the value accretion of the adviser. If it is determined that the result is less than a substantial value, the client should initiate a serious "meeting of the minds" with the adviser.

2. How does the client know that an adequate universe of buyers or sellers has been identified?
The adviser should define the universe of potential partners from the beginning of the process. Moreover, it may be appropriate for the adviser to cite examples of applicable buyers or sellers with whom they have worked in the past, either across the table or together. These issues will be addressed if the client performs adequate due diligence on the advisers under consideration. A level of comfort will be the outcome.

3. What are some requirements of advisers?
Predictably, advisers should be skilled in their representation, and the best way to illustrate this is through references, prior clients, and comparable situations. They should be transparent (as legally as possible) and not provide indefinite, albeit nebulous, examples. They should be clear and decisive with applicable contacts whom the client can reach.

4. What are some mandatory requisites for advisers?
The essential requirements include skill in identifying, eliminating, or presenting potential partners, and being that conduit, the buffer, on behalf of the client with the prospective partner. Knowing the partners and their universe is imperative. Equally critical is the adviser's ability to understand the products and services, overall makeup, financial performance history, and the culture of the client whom they are representing. These proficiencies

are fundamental and should be specifically demonstrated before they are engaged.

5. What risks should advisers assume?
Advisers to PE affiliation and other transactions should assume a certain amount of financial risk. The incentives entail upside remuneration when they do their job well. However, the client must be cooperative and provide adequate support so the adviser can do their job. Nonetheless, the risks that the advisers undertake include the extensive amount of time that working on this type of project will require. If the transaction fails, the adviser is at risk of receiving minimal fees for the time invested. These are the overriding risks to those advisers.

6. Should the selected adviser be an attorney?
Good legal counsel is imperative, whether it is for the buy-side or sell-side. Attorneys, like consultants, should stay in their lane. They should serve in the areas where they have expertise, which include the legal structuring and interpretations, and the compliance issues and other facets that may be a part of the transaction. However, attorneys generally do not serve best in buy-side or sell-side advisory services that would be better fulfilled by an investment banker, consultant, adviser, etc.

7. Should the selected adviser be specialized (i.e., knowledgeable in PE, hospital/health system, group mergers) specifically and exclusively?
No. The advisers should have a wide range of experience in doing deals involving all these entities. They should understand hospitals and health systems. If they are focused on a PE deal, they should apply, where applicable, that knowledge of how hospitals and health systems operate to the extent that they will supply a physician group with whom they are representing with needed information post-transaction, involving their relationship with that hospital or health system. So, while an adviser may only focus on representing a PE transaction, it is best that one be selected who understands and has done deals with all these parties, from hospitals to medical groups, *et al.*

8. What are the key criteria for selection?
Experience and a record of accomplishment, along with a reputation for getting deals done, are the main criteria. While basic and a matter of common sense, this is not always the case. Some advisers present themselves as

experienced and knowledgeable when they have little of these credentials. Further, some are within a firm that has all these aspects of experience and credentials, but the individuals proposed are inexperienced and unable to tap into (at least not enough) those experienced advisers within their firm. Therefore, prior to selection, the client should ask these tough questions and insist on specificity.

9. Should there be specific milestone requirements?

Absolutely. Milestones should be completed by the adviser, and prior to engagement on a more general basis. After engagement, such information should be provided more specifically. Markers in time should be used to determine the need for advanced and appropriate consultation within each milestone marker. Simultaneously, clients must be supportive of their advisers. They must equip them with timeline information and full disclosure of any positive and negative issues. Surprises should not exist after initial evaluation and due diligence by the adviser of the client.

10. Should a certain group of economic milestones be set?

Setting economic milestones is difficult because until the adviser has a good handle on the financial performance of the client, the EBITDA, and the multiples that the market would call for, it is difficult to hold them accountable for a specific financial milestone. After these milestones are better defined, however, financial milestones should be in place. IOIs and LOIs will be the first indicators of whether these milestones are being reached or not. This is the point to carefully assess the adviser and their role and function to date.

11. Should the adviser's approach and overall plan of assistance be documented in their engagement agreement?

Yes. Nevertheless, there are "forks in the road," and thus, there may be legitimate adjustments to the scope, even fees, based on things discovered during the entire process. Allowing the adviser to make certain adjustments when appropriate should be included.

12. Should the adviser name their actual team?

The firm's team of advisers should be completely transparent about their experience, credentials, and overall value. The adviser should explain and account for any changes that occur midstream.

13. Should the adviser be capable of completing the QofE and/or valuation calculations?

Although this capability is not mandatory, if the adviser does not have this ability within their firm, they should have another firm that is highly qualified for the client to consider. Ideally, the best adviser will be a "one-stop shop." Meaning they have the ability and expertise to provide all the services and do not parcel them out. Preferably, QofEs should be a skill. For hospitals, it is best for the advisory firm to be experienced in performing practical/healthcare entity appraisals.

14. Does the adviser need to be a registered broker-dealer?

No, but the key tenets of being a registered broker-dealer should be considered.

15. What are the key characteristics of legal counsel pertaining to a transaction?

As has been articulated, legal counsel should be skilled in all transactions related to the parties under consideration, whether hospitals/health systems, PE-backed firms, other groups, etc. These skills are imperative. Other necessary skills are an expert understanding or access to these skills in the firm of healthcare compliance and antitrust regulations.

16. What form of tax adviser would be best suited?

Similar to legal counsel and buy or sell-side advisers, the necessary skills should be experience in comparable deals and a thorough understanding of tax law related to the applicable transactions. Examples and references will be required.

17. How much applied knowledge is needed relative to the affiliation options?

The adviser's qualifications should encompass anecdotal, circumstantial, or just outright understanding from previous transactions overseen.

18. Should an adviser assume the role of adversary in negotiations? Should this be friendly or not?

The adviser can and should be the conduit for all negotiations. Often, they are the buffer. While they should not be adversarial, the adviser should stand firm on behalf of their client on the issues they represent, especially those that are challenging or problematic with the other side. The adviser who possesses these characteristics will earn their keep many times over.

19. What are the keys to measuring the success of an adviser?

Here are the key deliverables that must be attained:

- Achieve economic goals and objectives.
- Maintain relations, even with parties (such as hospitals) that are not a part of the alignment.
- Achieve long-term ROI (analogous to economic results noted above).
- Establish a "happy" and acceptable culture post-transaction.
- Set reasonable terms where neither party is resentful nor cynical about completing the transaction.
- Preserve the character of the current leadership, management, and governance, especially of a skilled, experienced, well-performed, and structured seller.

20. What are the keys to utilizing an adviser? Is an adviser always necessary?

The keys to using an adviser successfully are a combination of all the factors mentioned in this chapter and reiterated in the FAQs above. A good adviser will not only be justified but also pay significant dividends over a lengthy period. Most of the time, it is best to engage with some form or function of advisory assistance at the onset.

SUMMARY

Advisers are not an absolute necessity in every affiliation transaction. However, at the risk of sounding biased, we believe they are imperative in almost every situation, provided the party selected is skillful and experienced. Defining their roles, historical proficiency, and experience, and the specific deliverables expected of them, is imperative. Delineating the expectations, costs, and requirements is a necessary prerequisite before entering into a formal engagement.

REFERENCES

1. Securities Exchange Act of 1934. Pub L No. 73–291, 48 Stat. 881 (1934).
2. Guide to broker-dealer registration. U.S. Securities and Exchange Commission. April 2008. https://www.sec.gov/about/divisions-offices/division-trading-markets/division-trading-markets-compliance-guides/guide-broker-dealer-registration.

CHAPTER 12.

U.S. Healthcare Industry Status

PRIVATE EQUITY CAPITAL INVESTMENTS HAVE, by all measures, skyrocketed; this trend continues today. New deals are seemingly announced every week, while new players — on both the buy and sell sides — continue to enter the market, seeking transactions at all ends of the spectrum. And while volume fluctuates from month to month and year to year, this upward trend in healthcare PE deal volume does not appear to be waning anytime in the near future.

Private equity investment funds and PE-backed companies have been involved in this space for decades, and, of course, the industry has never been a stranger to merger and acquisition activity, as hospitals and health systems have been engaging in M&A transactions at least since the mid-20th century. So, let's take another look at what is really behind the growth in recent activity and discussion.

The regulatory requirements associated with healthcare services organizations have always been a key factor in transactions. For many years, regulatory challenges made private capital transactions in healthcare provider entities insurmountable in many cases. A central component here relates to laws and regulatory restrictions around the corporate practice of medicine, which regulates who is permitted to own equity in a medical provider entity, such as a medical practice, which traditionally is owned by clinical providers.

Further, it was difficult to paint a clear picture of the economic benefit for PE investors seeking to deploy capital. After all, if an investor is going to deploy millions — and in some cases hundreds of millions — of dollars, then there must be a clear return on investment plan and the value case for both investor and seller should be as well-defined as possible.

A primary reason for the recent growth in this space is due to the fact that investors have been more innovative in structuring deals where compelling value can be mapped and navigating the regulatory challenges that held back such deals in the past. Moreover, the industry itself has continued to become more intriguing due to the demographics and recession-resistant nature of the healthcare industry.

Most people now understand that while healthcare services come with many regulatory requirements and other challenges that are unique to this specific industry, such as continuously changing models in reimbursement, provider compensation, technology, and other niche industry dynamics, these services are not going away. Indeed, most healthcare specialties are expanding and growing at historic rates, due to technological innovation and clinical research. And as a result, the economic, or value, potential has also continued to grow.

In other chapters of this book, we investigate the various topics and unique dynamics related to PE investments in the healthcare services space, including several regulatory-related issues, economic and financial characteristics, and innovative approaches that come with an evolving industry landscape. IT is equally important to become familiar with the non-economic considerations involved in PE deals, as this can be one of the more overlooked components that buyers and, in particular, sellers do not often consider, compared to the financial aspects. After all, the valuation is typically the most focused-on element in most transactions. Nevertheless, it is common for the most significant challenges, both pre- and post-deal, to not be related to money at all. And among other nuanced topics, we will also look at future considerations, speculating on where this trend of PE in healthcare might potentially go in the coming years.

According to a report published in October 2025 by the Arkansas Center for Health Improvement (ACHI), there were 75 healthcare PE deals in 2012; in 2021, that number increased to over 480 transactions.[1] Much of the regulatory burdens that previously limited such deals from going through, specifically related to antitrust regulations, have in many ways decreased.

The National Institute for Health Care Management (NIHCM) released a report in 2022 that estimated more than 90% of healthcare PE transactions are exempt from federal antitrust regulatory review.[2] And, as the structures of these deals grow in complexity, particularly around ownership and equity models, understanding the ownership structures often put into place by PE sponsors can prove difficult for anyone looking into individual deals. The ACHI report mentioned previously stated, "While there have been hearings and legislative proposals at the federal level to stimulate greater transparency around private equity in healthcare, it is unclear whether meaningful federal action is likely to take place anytime soon."

Despite these evolving trends around the regulatory landscape involved in healthcare PE deals, the ACHI report pointed out that as of May 2025, approximately 35 states have introduced legislation and/or passed policy requiring hospitals, health systems, and private physician practices to notify authorities of "certain proposed transactions" involving private equity investors. The report adds that 15 of those states "regulate transactions that involve both nonprofit and for-profit healthcare entities."[2] Regulating PE transactions can pose challenges, however, because the size of the majority of these deals tends to fall below the mandatory federal reporting threshold, as outlined by the Federal Trade Commission (FTC), thus they are never reviewed from an antitrust perspective.

The industry and regulators have continued to focus on and monitor more closely a number of components of healthcare PE deals as new deals are announced. These components include the impact on the cost of care and patient access, the impact of consolidation on quality and outcomes, the ways utilization is changing, and geographic factors.

When looking at cost, for instance, the NIHCM report stated that after a PE deal is completed, data show increases in the amount charged per claim, as well as the maximum amount a health insurance plan will pay for a covered service. Studies have also shown that hospitals acquired by PE sponsors report increases in charge-to-cost ratios, referring to the amounts charged to payers and/or patients compared to the actual cost of providing the services involved. One study estimated a $71 increase in charges per claim on average when comparing PE-acquired practices across three specialties, versus average charges per claim for independent groups. Alternatively, some data show that costs improved. The NIHCM report cites a study that showed a $432 drop in costs per discharge for PE-backed provider organizations.[2]

The impact of consolidation is something closely monitored across all types of healthcare M&A deals, particularly those involving PE sponsors. Since PE investments in healthcare entities typically entail a "platform" investment that will grow through the continued acquisition of other entities, consolidating those providers and services under the platform anchor, this can significantly affect competition at both a local and broader geographic levels.

Generally speaking, consolidation in healthcare can result in increased prices and a negative impact on quality post-transaction, although this is not always the case. Still, consolidation will continue to affect the long-term outcomes associated with these deals and PE-backed healthcare provider organizations. According to the NIHCM study, "A study of 21 million Medicare beneficiaries with acute medical conditions found an association between PE-acquisition and significantly lower inpatient mortality and 30-day mortality among patients with acute myocardial infarction."[2]

What about the impact of PE deals on utilization? Some data suggest that due to the nature of PE investors' objective of maximizing revenue within a relatively short period of time (3–7 years), there is a risk of overutilization, where entities may increase unnecessary services and/or low-value care.

And finally, the geographic factors associated with healthcare PE deals also continue to play a role in this discussion. Expanding platforms will affect local and regional markets where services are expanded, which can have a downstream effect on those markets' overall capacity to provide services and care. This can create purchasing or contracting leverage through a "strength in numbers" scale strategy; however, this does not always come without disruptions in the continuum of care services from provider organizations within those markets.

The impact on local healthcare markets is an interesting trend to explore, particularly when PE-backed entities are involved. When pursuing a healthcare transaction, PE sponsors tend to follow a general model where an investor enters a market, expands in scale, scope, or both, then exits, typically within a 5–7-year timeline, if not shorter. This is occurring at every level and segment of the healthcare services industry, including all types and sizes of entities, as well as essentially all medical specialties and sub-specialties.

Zirui Song, an associate professor of health care policy at the Harvard Medical School, states, "Given the nature of its business model and the fragmented, often community-based structure of the delivery system, PE penetration into physician practices, procedural facilities, revenue cycle management (i.e., bill collection), health IT, and other areas ripe for consolidation will likely continue." Song goes on to explain that the policy landscape continues in the attempt to catch up with the industry's deal trends; though, private markets generally move at a pace that can make it difficult for the policy landscape to catch up with the ever-changing and evolving market dynamics.[2]

Ultimately, there is too much growth potential and untapped value in this space for the healthcare sector not to be a priority for capital investors seeking value and return. Further, the changing nature of healthcare delivery for the provider and the organizations they are a part of will only continue to make partnering with PE and PE-backed platforms more attractive.

However, it is important for all parties considering or actively pursuing transactions — whether now or in the future — to be cognizant of the various dynamics involved. In advising on countless transactions over the years, we can attest that no two transactions are exactly the same. Every deal has its unique dynamics and characteristics. However, there are a number of consistent themes or generalized characteristics that, if one has at least a basic understanding of, can be anticipated, such that unexpected issues can be avoided or addressed early in any deal process.

REFERENCES

1. Montgomery E. Private equity in health care. ACHI. October 2, 2025. Accessed January 5, 2026. https://achi.net/publications/private-equity-in-health-care/.
2. Zhu JM, Song Z. The growth of private equity in US health care: impact and outlook. NICHM Foundation. Accessed January 5, 2026. https://nihcm.org/publications/the-growth-of-private-equity-in-us-health-care-impact-and-outlook.

CHAPTER 13.
Group Mergers

With physician affiliations continually driven by a desire to improve quality and lower costs, one of the most common models is mergers. The "strength-in-numbers" concept continues to prevail and, some might argue, is more compelling today than ever. Physicians and physician leaders must adapt to ever-changing challenges, including reduced reimbursement, value-based payment models, increased costs, staffing challenges, and supply chain uncertainty. Responding to these issues and other challenges, alone or even in a small group, is daunting.

To address this concern, many physicians look at ways to increase their practice size. A greater number of providers working together can, in fact, mitigate many of the financial strains; additionally, more clinical expertise and diverse perspectives further enhance the appeal of a larger practice. For a variety of reasons, which we will discuss, merging practices is a common legal vehicle for such growth.

THE MERGER

The overview of legal and operational mergers described in the previous version remains accurate today. To clarify, legal and operational mergers are mechanically similar from a legal perspective. The difference, however, is the extent to which the merged practice combines its operations. At its core, a merger is one legal entity merging, by operation of law, into another legal entity. As Figure 13.1, below, shows, upon filing a Certificate of Merger with the applicable Secretary of State, one entity is completely absorbed by the surviving entity.

What allows merged physician practices to determine the extent of operational combination is the Stark law's definition of a "group practice." The Stark law allows subsets of physicians to be considered a single group practice if each subset consists of at least five physicians. Thus, while the legal operations of the merger result in one legal entity, the surviving entity can delineate profits and losses, revenues and expenses, and operations differently between "pods" of at least five physicians.

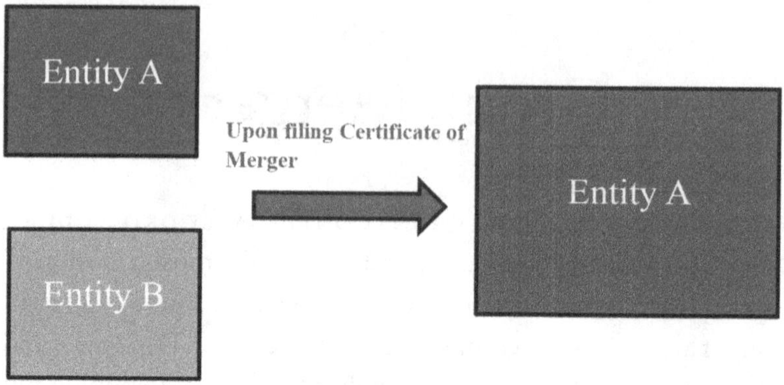

FIGURE 13.1. Filing a Certificate of Merger

It is worth underscoring that in a merger, the surviving entity assumes all the assets and liabilities of the merged entity. In healthcare, liabilities can be considerable due to historical billing practices. Therefore, entities considering a merger must carefully analyze the merged entity's historical billing practices and compliance with applicable reimbursement statutes, regulations, and payer requirements.

Additionally, the way payers, including enrollment in Medicare and most other governmental healthcare programs, treat a merger for enrollment purposes varies. See Figure 13.2 to assess the pros and cons. Awareness of this variance is critical.

Stock Purchase

One variation of the merger is a stock purchase agreement in which the acquiring entity purchases the target's stock, thereby making the target a wholly owned subsidiary of the acquiring entity. This structure is not commonly used in transactions with practices because it inherently keeps the practices separate, complicating integration. More importantly, it fails to satisfy the Stark law's group practice requirement of a single legal entity.

The Consolidation

While the stock purchase is not a convenient model for practice integration, in some circumstances, a different variation of the merger makes sense. Although rare, a consolidation is a type of merger in which two legal entities merge to form a new legal entity (Figure 13.3).

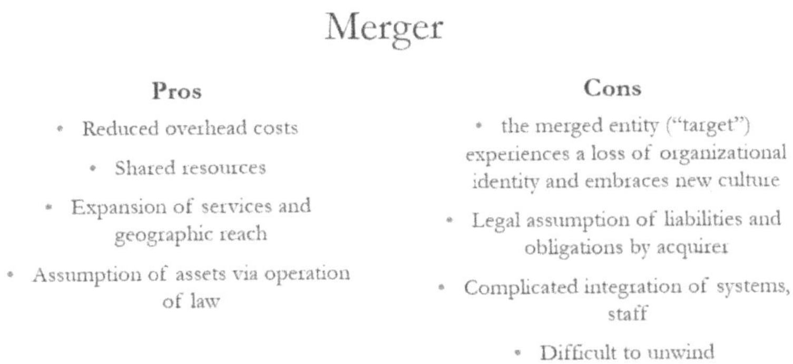

FIGURE 13.2. Common Pros and Cons Related to Mergers

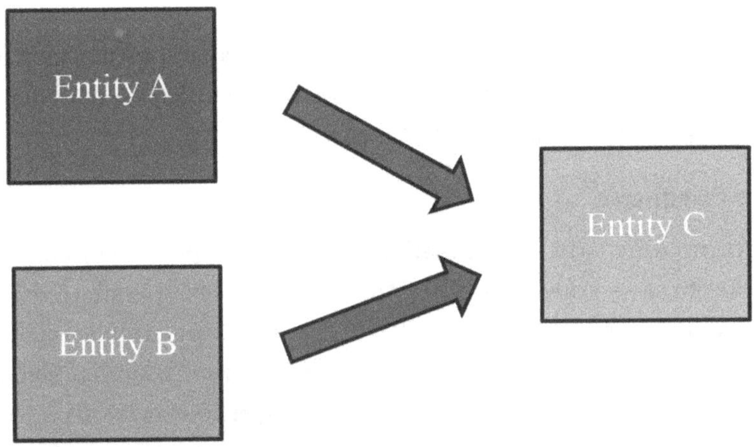

FIGURE 13.3. Consolidation Model

All the considerations common to a merger apply to a consolidation; however, the slight variation presents alternative pros and cons.

The consolidation model is fairly uncommon because payers, including enrollment in Medicare and most other governmental healthcare programs, treat a consolidation as a new enrollment, subject to all the new enrollment requirements, including credentialing and, possibly, survey. Despite this complication of new enrollment, the fact that the consolidated entity is "new" might allow, depending upon its structuring, the billing liabilities of each entity to remain with those legacy entities' tax identification numbers. CMS manuals describe a consolidation as a type of Change of Ownership (CHOW).

Consolidation

Pros

- New entity energy and excitement
- Entities begin with equal footing
- Most of the same pros as Merger

Cons

- Loss of organizational entity + legacy branding for both organizations
- Need for new tax-exempt determination
- New licensure
- Higher startup costs + timeline

FIGURE 13.4. Common Pros and Cons Related to Consolidation

Given the liability considerations inherent in mergers and consolidations, many physician leaders and their advisers prefer to utilize an asset purchase structure to "merge" practices (See Figure 13.5).

Asset Purchase

More commonly than not, affiliations of physician practices occur via an asset purchase — especially when the two practices operate in the same specialty and within the same market area. When operating as such, both practices typically have similar contracting needs, with similar electronic medical record vendors, supply vendors, and payer contracts with specialty-specific rate schedules. Thus, the acquiring entity may not need to assume contracts and provider enrollments of the acquired entity, as they would be duplicative.

Under an asset purchase, the acquiring entity purchases specific assets from the target for fair market value (which is commonly determined by a valuation firm that is hired by the parties). Since most contracts and enrollments are not necessary, the assets typically involve real estate or leaseholder interests, fixed furniture and equipment, workforce in place, and specific contracts. Additionally, the physicians of the target, especially the shareholder physicians, negotiate employment agreements and shareholder agreements for their future provision of professional services as members of the acquiring entity. These agreements are key considerations in an asset transaction, especially if the parties intend to consolidate operations rather than utilize the "pod" model described above.

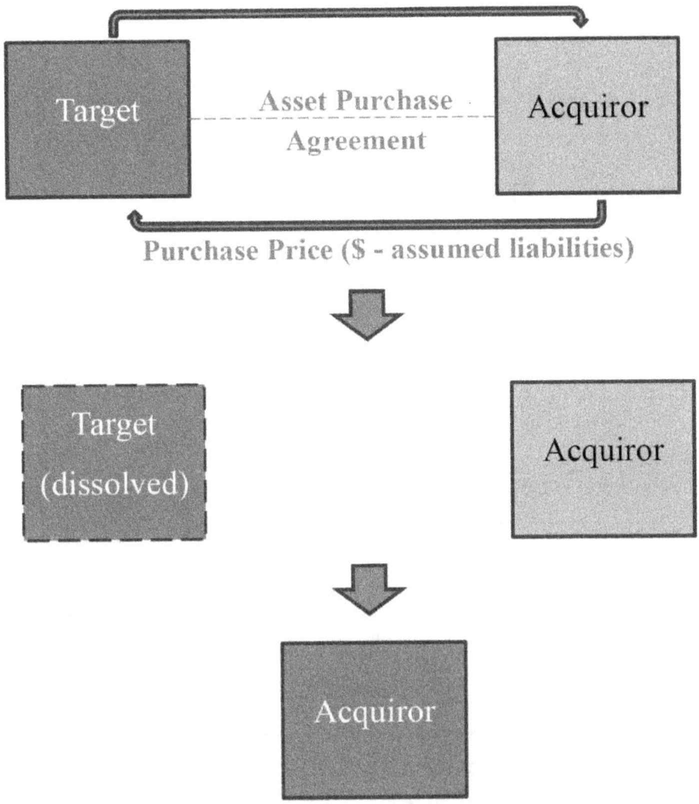

FIGURE 13.5. Using an Asset Purchase Structure to "Merge" Practices

As depicted, the target receives cash or other monetary consideration in exchange for the transfer of assets to the acquiror. Depending on how the parties structure the transfer of accounts receivable of the target, the target may "work" its AR after the transaction, which creates additional cash. Cash from AR, along with the transaction consideration, is thereafter used to pay all of the outstanding debts of the target, and the remaining proceeds are distributed to its shareholders. Figure 13.6 presents the pros and cons of the asset purchase model

As mentioned, the acquiring entity does not commonly assume the payer's contracts or governmental enrollments of the target. However, payer contracts increasingly include provisions that allow the payer to review the provider agreements of the two entities involved in an asset purchase if both are enrolled and decide whether the two provider agreements will be

Asset Purchase

Pros	Cons
Flexible structure–can choose what assets and liabilities are transferred, and what remains with the target	If all assets of THC are acquired, entity will likely be dissolved or repurposed
The target can continue to exist, albeit in a repurposed fashion	Most complicated reassignment of 3rd party contracts and licenses
Structure most commonly associated with purchase price	Typically, the greatest loss of control by target

FIGURE 13.6. Common Pros and Cons Related to Asset Purchases

honored after the acquisition. Careful consideration of the terms of these provider agreements is essential to understanding the economic effect of the transaction.

From an enrollment perspective, most asset purchases result in the acquiring entity simply adding the target's operations as new practice locations on the acquiring entities' enrollment forms and applications. This process is much more streamlined than undergoing a CHOW or creating new enrollments and thus is preferred. Keep in mind, however, that state licensure for specific practice types and equipment will also be impacted, each with its own transfer process. Furthermore, since the equipment and operations subject to such licensure are not transferred by operation of law as they are in a merger, the regulatory licensure process is typically more complicated in asset acquisitions.

Considering the varying legal models that can be used to merge practices is a key component of strategic decision-making. The processes are unique and offer varying advantages and disadvantages, helping physicians and physician leaders determine which model aligns most with the goals of the transaction. Understanding the assets, liabilities, and operations of the practices, along with the goals and strategy underscoring the transaction, requires diligence, which, in turn, highlights factors for the leaders to consider when determining which structure is best to merge practices.

CHAPTER 14.

Transactions Update: Nature of Affiliation Transactions

THROUGHOUT THIS BOOK, WE HAVE GONE to great lengths to provide insights into the various players involved in these transactions, the models and structures, and the emotional, psychological, and mental frameworks. As we wind down, we examine and elaborate on the nuances of the approach and completion of transactions from the perspectives of key representative entities: medical practices, hospitals and health systems, clinically integrated networks (CINs), and private equity (PE)-backed firms, along with other for-profit investor structures.

STEP-BY-STEP APPROACH

In most instances, the transaction process includes a period of initial contact and discussions, definition of structure and affiliation models, due diligence, and operational overview, culminating in negotiations and structuring of the legal agreements that support the affiliation. Advisers may educate their respective clients throughout the process.

As we consider these affiliation transactions and how best to reach a transaction closing, we must keep in mind the typical phases or stages of review:

1. Evaluate the options.
2. Test the water.
3. Consider realistic structures' economic terms.
4. Segue to meet ultimate goals and objectives.
5. Continue to educate and communicate.
6. Complete operational review and due diligence, including reverse due diligence.
7. Review economic terms and complete an indication of interest (IOI)/letter of intent (LOI).
8. Negotiate the economics and other terms of the transaction.
9. Acquaint the key players with the process and keystone issues.

10. Consider the "snags" inherent to each transaction.

After completing all the above, take a break to acquaint all owners of the sell-side entity, plus all other matters and potential inhibitors, before moving ahead with closing.

SPECIFIC APPROACHES TO TRANSACTIONS

The process of working toward a transaction in specific installments of responsibilities and initiatives is similar regardless of whether the entity is a hospital or health system, PE or practices, or other related healthcare investors. Each party may have varying degrees of complexity, but overall, they are quite similar, as summarized in Figure 14.1.

FIGURE 14.1. Specific Approaches and Transactions

Specific Approaches and Transactions	Action Steps
1. Review the likely structure of affiliation.	Decide early on as to the structure and educate all involved parties.
2. Consider typical terms and conditions.	Share examples and key parameters of the affiliation strategies/structures.
3. Analyze EBITDA multiples, rollover, income scrape, if applicable, and other market-based conclusions.	Complete the financial analyses incumbent on the selected affiliation structure.
4. Conclude on a universe of interested buyers/affiliation partners.	Provide a summary of workable parties; do not overstate.
5. Recap terms for management and employees, as applicable.	Outline these non-economic terms along with other terms.
6. Define the terms of the agreement, including other specific parameters and boundaries.	Reach an understanding of these key points as early as possible.
7. Decide termination and unwind provisions.	Address these provisions, even though the hope is that they are improbable.
8. Depending on the structure undertaken and the affiliation partner, ascertain the platform and growth plans.	Complete at the proper time but not too soon; complete the deal at hand first.
9. Consider older versus younger physicians and their preferences.	Know these characteristics and the subsequent challenges early on and decide how best to address them.
10. Review restrictive covenant terms and conditions.	Define parameters quickly; do not wait for most other matters of reconciliation.

While Figure 14.1 outlines in a general sense these key matters within affiliation transactions, some are more applicable than others. For example, PE affiliation would apply to all of those matters in Figure 14.1; affiliation with hospitals and health systems would most likely not consider all of these listed.

HOSPITALS AND HEALTH SYSTEMS

Affiliating with hospitals and health systems, primarily focused on medical groups, varies in their structures and the degree of alignment. Consider Figure 4.1 in Chapter 4, as much of it pertains to hospitals and health systems' affiliation with medical groups and other healthcare entities. No matter the level of affiliation, limited, moderate, or full, the overarching points listed in Figure 14.2 should be considered.

FIGURE 14.2. Affiliation Characteristics and Considerations

Affiliation Characteristics and Considerations	How Best to Address
1. Consider realistic and viable partners.	This point applies to medical groups and other healthcare provider entities with hospitals or health systems that are a fit compared to various issues, traits, and prior connections between the hospital and the medical group/healthcare entity.
2. Define structure and services.	This consideration is about whether the model is limited, moderate, full, or a combination of several, all of which could be possible. For example, something as simple as "call" compensation to a much more complex full alignment model, such as a professional services agreement (PSA), is subject to consideration and review, then coordination within the proper transaction structure.
3. Consider models of affiliation.	Again, this concern refers to the various models or combinations, listed in Figure 4.1 in Chapter 4.
4. Review economics.	The economics of any transaction are essential, not only from a return on investment (ROI) standpoint, but also as a means to provide incentives for the parties to align and affiliate. Fair market value (FMV) and other compliance standards must be met.

(figure continues)

FIGURE 14.2. Affiliation Characteristics and Considerations

Affiliation Characteristics and Considerations	How Best to Address
5. Consider post-transaction governance.	Post-transaction governance is a significant consideration as to who and at what level of leadership and development of decision-making will apply. Usually, hospitals or health systems want to stay in control and have the final say in these matters. The winds of change have, to some extent, given more power and decision-making (governance) to physician groups. Hospitals/health systems are typically in ultimate control with reserved powers.
6. Consider post-transaction leadership.	Leadership, particularly clinical and medical director leadership, is a critical consideration. Physicians should maintain a prominent level of leadership within alignment structures.
7. Review ancillary investment opportunities.	The ability for physicians who align and affiliate with hospitals and health systems to also have a share of the ancillaries applicable to their specialty has become a major goal. This is largely a reason for practices and physicians to affiliate with hospitals and health systems. Always keeping compliance and related concerns in mind, these affiliations often take the form of joint equity ventures and provide much incentive for a long-term working relationship.
8. Consider facilities and real estate.	Akin to joint ventures and ancillaries are physical clinical facilities, surgery centers, medical office buildings, and others, which offer opportunities.
9. Consider personnel and staffing.	Affiliating with hospitals and health systems inevitably involves a complete practice entity, including the clinical and administrative staff. These staff members should be carefully considered within the structure and affiliation transaction. Benefits are also of major significance in such formations.
10. Assess term and termination rights.	The ability to end the relationship within certain parameters is of major importance in these transactions. Hospitals and health systems want the protection of some security, as do physicians. These issues should be a part of the transactional negotiations.
11. Review restrictive covenants.	Hospitals prefer placing some form of restriction on a practice if the affiliation strategy unwinds. The hospital looks to limit the physicians' ability to align with a competitor. The hospital often allows the private practice to return to private practice if a competing hospital or health system is not involved.

(figure continues)

FIGURE 14.2. Affiliation Characteristics and Considerations

Affiliation Characteristics and Considerations	How Best to Address
12. Address compensation.	The physicians are interested in how their compensation is structured. Usually, this is a combination of a base guaranteed pay for a certain period, or the continuation of the entire contract. In addition, incentives tied to productivity are often based on work RVU production. Further, quality-based incentive pools are usually a part of the compensation equation. Other specific areas of incentives may be included within the compensation structure.
13. Establish legal and regulatory agreements.	Beyond compliance issues, the parties must have strong legal agreements that define all terms and conditions.
14. Establish a compliance plan.	Akin to regulatory adherence is having a comprehensive compliance plan that is transferred to the physician group once aligned with the hospital and health system.
15. Structure wraparounds.	Wraparounds are any form of affiliation that is "wrapped around" the basic core model, usually a full alignment model, such as employment or PSA. These wraparounds should be structured properly, in terms of compliance and economic issues.
16. Consider the unwind.	The unwind is not often considered because of the lack of expectation of need. Contrary to this thinking, unwinding happens fairly often and is a matter to consider.

GROUP MERGERS

When physicians consider their opportunities for affiliation, many prefer to align with other physicians, absent PE and hospitals and health systems. Usually, these affiliations entail a group merger, but they could align with a jointly owned management services organization (MSO) or ancillary entity such as an ambulatory surgery center. Many of the same characteristics apply within group mergers; however, merging groups is more complex because all merger partners have a go-forward stake in all these areas.

When merging groups, typically there are 25–30 issues to consider and resolve within the merger process. These issues require careful consideration and negotiations that include the parties confronting and reconciling the issues prior to the merger's closing.

Some groups adopt the philosophy that mergers should take place first, and the parties can work out the details of these issues later. We disagree and believe that all issues of consequence should be settled before the closing. A list of these issues, many of which have been considered within other transaction themes discussed above, is presented in Figure 14.3.

FIGURE 14.3. Issues to Consider When Merging Groups

Issue	Summary
1. Organizational Structure.	This issue refers to the post-transaction working relationship, but more so, the legal organizational structure, post-transaction.
2. Organization Name.	Depending on the affiliation structure, the collaborative entity may require a new name.
3. Valuation/Equity Values.	This issue would not apply until formal consolidation.
4. Capitalization of New Group.	There is usually a need to invest some additional money to support whatever form of affiliation is needed.
5. Other Major Assets Owned.	These assets usually pertain to the equipment associated with ancillary services, depending on the organizational structure.
6. Other Ventures.	These ventures require further discussion and full disclosure to avoid conflicts of interest and other financial ramifications for either or both groups, as income that is a threat to the other. An example is when either party faces a competitive threat to the other. Think of a carved-out PSA for that merger partner to perform services for the hospital that would later present a conflict for the newly merged group. Another example is ownership in an ancillary surgery center.
7. Governance.	Governance is especially important and requires thorough, detailed discussion points. There should be a clear understanding and agreement relating to governance, post-affiliation. This matter would depend upon the overall transaction and related structural setup.
8. Call.	This may not be as relevant (particularly at the beginning) unless the two groups overlap in their hospital coverage.
9. Information Technology (IT) Systems.	IT is critical to the success of the newly aggregated entity. Typically, it is best to have a common IT platform, though there are ways to work around the matter (at least initially), depending on the overall structure of the collaborative effort.

(figure continues)

FIGURE 14.3. Issues to Consider When Merging Groups

Issue	Summary
10. Administrative Leadership/ Management.	Like governance, leadership is essential to define and agree on the day-to-day management and leadership structures going forward.
11. Centralized Billing Office (CBO).	The CBO gets to more granular areas of consideration for future collaboration. While combining the revenue cycle (and specifically, the billing office) functions may not be one of the primary goals of such collaboration, it is a major area of consolidation and a cost savings opportunity.
12. Internal Accounting.	Likewise, this issue may vary, depending upon the structure and needs of the affiliation.
13. Staffing.	Both clinical and administrative staffing will be a key area of discussion, and lines will need to be drawn as to responsibilities of oversight and management, similar to the administrative management function (see number 10 above).
14. Legal Counsel.	Usually, both entities will have legal representation, combining it into a single representation, post-transaction.
15. Physical Practice Sites.	Collaborative efforts are typically considered as a way to save on costs, and physical sites may be combined. If sites are leased (as they usually are), this will not happen immediately and must be considered in the overall pro forma financial projections pertaining to the potential transaction.
16. Benefits.	The assumption is that the merged structure's benefits will be applied as a group.
17. Buy-In/Buyout Provisions.	As the groups merge, there should be definitive discussions and agreement about how partners are added and removed as equity holders. Moreover, the fundamental discussion of how individuals become partners within the merged entity should be considered. The buy-in relates to the comments above, particularly, "grandfathering" of individuals into the partnership roles, and whether there is an actual financial buy-in is an issue to consider. As discussed above, buyouts should be considered, but more in the context of whether there would be pay-outs to the physicians prior to the merger. Buyouts should be considered, but more in the context of whether there would be pay-outs for the physicians prior to merging relative to their former group.

(figure continues)

FIGURE 14.3. Issues to Consider When Merging Groups

Issue	Summary
20. Accounts Receivable (A/R) at the Time of Merger.	Usually, this is straightforward, and each group retains and collects its existing A/R.
21. Consolidation of Practices and Other Processes.	This relates to the fundamental and systemic discussion relative to the goals and objectives of the overall collaborative efforts.
22. Marketing Plan/ Name Branding.	Marketing should be a primary reason for the collaborative affiliation efforts; that is, to combine referral sources, name recognition, and branding.
23. Income Distribution Plan (IDP).	The IDP is one of the most important and potentially time-consuming and stressful issues. Depending on their agreed-upon organizational affiliation, the groups may best operate under the same IDP, though if maintaining separate divisions, this matter may not be absolute. With joint ancillary services and certain areas of overhead and services like central business office combined, it will become increasingly challenging to operate under separate IDPs. We recommend common IDPs.

CLINICALLY INTEGRATED NETWORKS (CINS)

CINs are more than a payer contracting mechanism; clinical integration and CINs can allow for even more affiliation structures, such as MSOs and other transactional combinations. One of the common major snags in forming an effective CIN is the capital required for the CIN to be clinically integrated. Therefore, the capital is often supplied by health systems, which maintain control and authority over the governance, leadership, and other major matters. They also control the payer contracting, which is probably best because the hospital or health system has more influence over payer rates, even though hospitals are often more concerned about payer rates on inpatient and related services than ambulatory and clinic (i.e., practice) professional fees.

Some CINs are closed in that they require the participants to only contract with payers through the CIN or only with prominent payers. These matters should be considered as the CIN is formed and its bylaws and overall goals and objectives are articulated. Physician groups can become a part of a CIN but must be clinically integrated, which means sharing clinical data and other supporting materials. They may be reticent to do so because of their lack of overall trust in the health system. Much of this stems from years of separation and a lack of collegiality.

SUMMARY

It is imperative to consider these key issues prior to the actual transaction. Likewise, it is essential to fully define differences evaluated and reconciled so there are limited conflicts in the future, post-transaction. A clear understanding of terms will avert unwinds and/or major conflicts going forward. Defining the leadership, governance, economic terms, legal parameters, etc., is essential to these transactions, no matter the players involved.

CHAPTER 15.

Legal and Regulatory Considerations

SEVERAL WELL-DEFINED REGULATORY STRUCTURES, such as the physician self-referral law (Stark), the concept of relative value units in establishing physician compensation, the anti-kickback statute (AKS), and other key regulatory schemes, focus on the results of an affiliation. Rather than providing updates to these structures, this chapter centers on legal and regulatory considerations involved in the process of affiliations, notably mergers.

While Stark, AKS, and other laws are relevant to mergers, antitrust laws and HIPAA have applicability to the merger process itself. Additionally, brief attention is given to recently enacted value-based care exceptions and safe harbors to highlight the increasing importance of quality care and opportunities that merged physician practices may consider related thereto.

ANTITRUST CONSIDERATIONS

When physician practices merge, especially if they are of the same medical specialty, the resulting practice must be analyzed for antitrust compliance. While the Trump administration appears to have relaxed President Biden's aggressive enforcement of antitrust laws, the rapidly increasing size of the U.S. healthcare industry continues to demand regulatory attention.

The Federal Trade Commission (FTC) and the Department of Justice (DOJ) scrutinize healthcare consolidations and joint ventures more closely as a means of ensuring healthy competition with the goal of reducing the overall cost of healthcare. The FTC and DOJ commonly use the Herfindahl-Hirschman Index (HHI) to assess market concentration, which mathematically calculates the impact a merger will have on a particular market's concentration. The FTC tends to focus on insurance, pharmaceuticals, and consumer protection issues, whereas the DOJ is focused on physician mergers and particularly on compliance with Section 7 of the Clayton Act.

Mergers of physician practices are typically evaluated based on the medical specialty as the "product." Additionally, the destinations to which patients will travel to obtain replacement "products" are used to establish the relevant geographic market. Physician mergers that may result in increased market concentration receive more regulatory scrutiny due to the perceived corresponding increase in bargaining power with insurers, employers, and patients.

Thus, it is important for physicians to understand how a potential merger may affect a relevant geographic market to determine whether such a merger is likely to receive scrutiny from the DOJ or FTC, even if a Hart-Scott-Rodino (HSR) Act notification is not required.

HSR established the federal pre-merger notification program. Parties to mergers or acquisitions that meet the filing threshold must notify the FTC and DOJ to provide these agencies with information regarding each party's business and the proposed deal. Most mergers of physician practices are unlikely to require an HSR filing because the filing threshold, at the time of this publication, is required for transactions valued in excess of $126.5 million.

While the federal agencies are most likely to scrutinize large physician practice mergers, states are becoming increasingly involved in healthcare antitrust regulation through their attorneys general. When state regulating agencies view factors such as market consolidation, barriers to entry, and effects on pricing, they do so through a state lens. Given this perspective and the large federal HSR filing threshold, states are likely to be more concerned about physician practice mergers than the federal government.

As states become more involved in scrutinizing healthcare acquisitions, they are enacting laws modeled after the federal HSR to be able to review transactions that fall below the federal reporting threshold. These laws are commonly referred to as "mini-HSRs" or "baby HSRs." These laws may require companies to file state premerger notifications under certain circumstances that would not require notification under federal rules. California, Colorado, Connecticut, Hawaii, Illinois, Massachusetts, Minnesota, Nevada, New Hampshire, New York, Oregon, Rhode Island, and Washington have already implemented such laws.

Given the increased attention on the healthcare industry as a whole, professional entities should consider antitrust concerns in transactions.

Counsel can help structure transactions to avoid or mitigate the risk that may result in scrutiny from federal or state regulatory agencies.

HIPAA

Privacy of medical information has always been a concern for physicians as their fiduciary relationship to patients requires a heightened level of confidentiality. States have historically relied on this fiduciary relationship to protect patient information; however, the federal Health Insurance Portability and Accountability Act of 1996 (HIPAA)[1] and its implementing regulations changed the regulatory environment for the privacy and security of individually identifiable health information, or protected health information (PHI), forever.

In the merger context, practices must be allowed to share their patients' health information at some point in the transaction. The timing of such sharing should take into account antitrust concerns and HIPAA compliance. In addition, as practice mergers become increasingly complex and involve more financial risk, practices involved in a merger seek advisory support from lawyers, consultants, accountants, and others. These third parties must also have access to the PHI of each practice involved in the merger and must obtain such in compliance with HIPAA and relevant state laws.

The federal preamble to the HIPAA Final Privacy Rule speaks to the disclosure of PHI in diligence. Ultimately, HIPAA allows practices to disclose PHI to each other for diligence as a part of each party's healthcare operations, provided the parties have executed a common confidentiality agreement that requires destruction or return of data if the transaction does not close.

However, this discussion does not involve disclosures to third parties, such as lawyers, consultants, and accountants, as mentioned above. Therefore, each party to the merger must enter into business associate agreements with such third parties, assuming they are providing a service that qualifies them as a business associate, prior to the disclosure of PHI.

Thus, while HIPAA compliance is an element of due diligence in a merger, it also demands compliance in the process of diligence itself. Compliance with HIPAA in this context is not terribly complicated, but it does require attention to detail to ensure appropriate disclosure, including disclosing only the minimum amount of PHI necessary to accomplish the purpose of the requested disclosure.

REGULATORY EXCEPTIONS AND SAFE HARBORS

Under President Trump's first administration, the Department of Health and Human Services (HHS) embarked on a "regulatory sprint to coordinated care" in an effort to remove regulatory obstacles. In notable rulemaking from December 2020, HHS published three new exceptions to the Stark Law for arrangements involving differing levels of risk within value-based arrangements, and the OIG for HHS published similar AKS safe harbors.

Stark Law – Value-Based Care Exceptions

The Physician Self-Referral Law, Section 1877 of the Social Security Act (42 U.S.C. 1395nn),[2] commonly called the Stark law, prohibits a physician from making referrals of designated health services payable by Medicare and Medicaid to an entity with which the physician or an immediate family member has a financial relationship unless an exception is met. The law also prohibits filing claims with Medicare for any designated healthcare services improperly referred.

Three new exceptions to the Stark law's referral prohibition were promulgated at the end of 2020 to encourage coordinated care. 42 C.F.R. 411.357(aa)(1) describes payments to physicians in value-based arrangements that take on full financial risk, such as capitated payments from payers or full financial responsibility for the total care of a patient population.

Given the inherent nature of the assumption of full financial risk, much latitude was given by HHS to the structure of such compliant arrangements. Subsection (2) describes arrangements where physicians take on at least 10% of the financial risk. Such arrangements have more compliance requirements than those described in subsection (1), but more flexibility is afforded than most prior exceptions, including the lack of a requirement that the payments be consistent with fair market value. The arrangements envisioned by subsection (2) appear to be clinical co-management and service line arrangements, among others. Finally, subsection (3) describes value-based arrangements that do not take on any financial risk. These arrangements have the most regulatory requirements, including a written description of the outcome measure to be achieved by the value-based activity carried out by the physician, given the lack of financial risk assumed, and they can be good considerations for arrangements between physicians and unaffiliated hospitals.

Violation of Stark may result in potentially financially devastating sanctions and civil liability. First, regardless of the intent of the violating party, no payment shall be given for an arrangement that violates the Stark law, so the service would be provided at the expense of the healthcare provider. Second, if the violator knows or should have known that an improper claim was submitted, then that violator shall be subject to a civil penalty of up to $15,000 for each such service. Third, if the violator entered an arrangement or scheme for which the violator knows or should have known that the principal purpose was assuring referrals by a physician in violation of the Stark law, then the violator shall be subject to a civil penalty of up to $100,000 for each arrangement. Given the strict liability nature of the Stark law, adherence to all elements of an applicable exception is necessary to establish compliance and avoid these significant penalties.

These exceptions to the Stark law create financial opportunities for physicians that typically increase as the size of physician practices grows and the quality of care improves.

AKS – Value-Based Care Safe Harbors

The anti-kickback statute, 42 U.S.C. 1320a-7b(b),[3] prevents anyone, including physicians, healthcare providers, or healthcare suppliers, from receiving remuneration for referring patients to another physician, healthcare provider, or healthcare supplier when that patient is covered by a federal healthcare program such as Medicare or Medicaid.

Courts have interpreted referral under the AKS to include requests by a physician for a consultation with another physician, requests, or establishment of a plan of care by a physician which includes the provision of health services, and the certifying or recertifying of the need for any health service for which payment may be made under a federal healthcare service.

The AKS requires that a referral be made and that remuneration be paid for the referral. Remuneration is not simply the payment of money for the referral. Instead, remuneration is the receipt of anything of value in exchange for a referral, such as the payment of rent, new equipment, or even the performance of services. Given the breadth of the AKS' application, the Office of Inspector General for the Department of Health and Human Services, which enforces the AKS, has promulgated a number of safe harbors.

Remuneration received as a component of certain common arrangements will not be treated as a criminal offense under the AKS, if the arrangement squarely satisfies every element of an applicable safe harbor. The safe harbors are an extensive list of permissible arrangements that will be immune from scrutiny, if properly satisfied. Recently, outcomes-based payment arrangements have been included in the personal services and management contracts safe harbor, and specific value-based care safe harbors have been developed.

In accordance with 42 C.F.R. 1001.952(d)(2), physicians may receive an outcomes-based payment if the physician achieves one or more legitimate outcome measures that are selected based on credible medical support and have benchmarks that are used to quantify improvements in or the maintenance of quality care or reductions in cost. These outcomes-based payment arrangements need to meet additional requirements of the safe harbor, including being written in an agreement with a term of at least one year, being consistent with fair market value, involving regular monitoring of the physician's performance, and periodically assessing the impact of the benchmark on its clinical or financial purpose. Of note, pharmaceutical manufacturers, pharmacy benefit managers, laboratory companies, DME providers and certain other types of entities are not allowed to participate in an outcomes-based payment arrangement, or the other value-based care arrangements that follow.

In accordance with 42 C.F.R. 1001.952(ee), a value-based enterprise (VBE) may provide remuneration to a participant in the VBE. Subsection (ff) allows a VBE to provide payments and things of value to a VBE participant in arrangements involving substantial downside risk. In addition to a number of requirements, the VBE must take on substantial downside risk, which equates to 20% or 30% of the total losses for a patient population on an annual basis. Additionally, the VBE participant must take on a meaningful share of such risk, which roughly equates to 5% of the downside and upside risk of the VBE or enter a capitated payment model for the participant's provision of goods or services.

Subsection (gg) allows VBEs to provide remuneration to its participants who are engaged in full financial risk models, meaning that the VBE has assumed full financial responsibility for a payer's patient population for at least a one-year period. Certain elements must be met, as further described in this subsection, but the fact that full financial risk is borne by the VBE and, in turn, its participants inherently allows for flexibility in the arrangement. Subsection (hh) allows certain entities to provide patient engagement tools and support to patients to encourage their engagement with value-based initiatives of the VBE. The value of such tools and support cannot exceed $500 annually, which is adjusted annually. This safe harbor allows VBE to incentivize patients, thereby increasing their accountability for their own care, and connecting the final dot in the value-based care network.

It is important to understand that the AKS imposes criminal liability. Thus, a violation of the law could result in fines, imprisonment for up to 10 years, and exclusion from federal healthcare program participation. Fines can amount to up to $50,000 per kickback and three times the amount of remuneration provided. Thus, it is imperative that physician practices thoroughly review value-based arrangements for compliance with the safe harbors to ensure compliance in this evolving area of healthcare payment.

SUMMARY

Physician practices embarking on the merger process must give considerable attention to the legal and regulatory compliance of each practice in their diligence, but they must also conduct the merger in a compliant manner, which this chapter sought to present. Additionally, an increasingly important metric of success will be the quality of care provided by physicians and their practitioners. Practices considering merging must undertake measures to understand the quality of care each provides, and may be able to develop arrangements, in compliance with Stark law and AKS, that allow the merged practice to take greater advantage of their value-based care models.

REFERENCES

1. HIPAA Statute. PUBLIC LAW 104–191—AUG. 21, 1996. Accessed April 30, 2026. PLAW-104publ191.pdf https://www.hhs.gov/hipaa/for-professionals/privacy/laws-regulations/index.html. The Standards for Privacy of Individually

Identifiable Health Information ("Privacy Rule") establishes, for the first time, a set of national standards for the protection of certain health information. The U.S. Department of Health and Human Services ("HHS") issued the Privacy Rule to implement the requirement of the Health Insurance Portability and Accountability Act of 1996 ("HIPAA").[1] The Privacy Rule standards address the use and disclosure of individuals' health information — called "protected health information" by organizations subject to the Privacy Rule — called "covered entities," as well as standards for individuals' privacy rights to understand and control how their health information is used. Within HHS, the Office for Civil Rights ("OCR") has responsibility for implementing and enforcing the Privacy Rule with respect to voluntary compliance activities and civil money penalties.

2. The Stark Law, codified at 42 U.S.C. § 1395nn, prohibits physicians from referring Medicare or Medicaid patients to entities for designated health services if they or their immediate family members have a financial relationship, unless an exception applies. Accessed April 30, 2026. https://www.bing.com/ck/a?!&&p=451a11b3d4a93f9c93c7ecd7ada431d9c993e43aea90f6e479cd0a50f70f467bJmltdHM9MTc3NzUwNzIwMA&ptn=3&ver=2&hsh=4&fclid=027627ba-46e2-612d-0fa9-31894782608b&psq=Stark+law+statute&u=a1aHR0cHM6Ly9uYXRsYXdyZXZpZXcuY29tL2FydGljbGUvZG9udC1sZXQtc3RhcmstbGF3LWNhdGNoLXlvdS1ndWFyZC1yaXNrLXJlbWFpbnMtZGVzcGl0ZS1sdWxs
3. Anti-kickback Statute. Accessed April 30, 2026. Anti-Kickback Statute [42 U.S.C. § 1320a-7b(b)]. The AKS is a criminal law that prohibits the knowing and willful payment of "remuneration" to induce or reward patient referrals or the generation of business involving any item or service payable by the Federal health care programs (e.g., drugs, supplies, or health care services for Medicare or Medicaid patients). Remuneration includes anything of value and can take many forms besides cash, such as free rent, expensive hotel stays and meals, and excessive compensation for medical directorships or consultancies. In some industries, it is acceptable to reward those who refer business to you. However, in the Federal health care programs, paying for referrals is a crime. The statute covers the payers of kickbacks — those who offer or pay remuneration — as well as the recipients of kickbacks — those who solicit or receive remuneration. Each party's intent is a key element of their liability under the AKS.

CHAPTER 16.

What Is Next and Where Do We Go from Today?

As we conclude this book on physician affiliation strategies, we hope some areas of transactions have become clearer. Still, there are outstanding questions. Going forward, healthcare services will continue to expand and become a greater concern for the general populace. More young adults will seek career opportunities in healthcare, in both clinical and nonclinical professions and vocations. They will look for opportunities to enjoy a lucrative career and find satisfaction in contributing to healing sicknesses and diseases.

Let us pause and reflect on the present and look into the future through that proverbial crystal ball. No matter the emphasis — clinical, administrative, financial, managerial — there are significant issues to address. These include:

1. **Economics**. Revenue and reimbursement from third-party payers, both governmental and commercial, will continue to be the greatest concern. Bending the cost curve is essential. With increasing technology and overall consumer expectations, including the cost of research and development, equipment, and provider compensation, economic concerns will lead the way.

   What can we do to develop the best possible results along with the best quality of care? This question is difficult to answer. Some want continued economic and financial windfalls emanating from the hard work, dedication, and technical expertise that healthcare services both provide and require. Others are more benevolent and realize that there is always a degree of human kindness and care, no matter the cost or the reimbursement. The intersection of quality of care and economics will continue to cause concern and demand reconciliation.
2. **Quality of Care**. At the heart of our U.S. healthcare industry is healing the sick and caring for all patients, regardless of their ability to pay. This mission will continue, although the increase in free and indigent

care will further strain the entire system and inevitably result in less financial success for hospitals, health systems, physicians, and private investors. While state and federal government entities may accept more of the responsibility, they will resort to their only source of revenue: taxpayers.

3. **Payers.** Governmental and commercial payers have limitations and will continue to express those limitations on what they can reimburse, both employer-sponsored health plans and their direct patient payment relationships. The federal government is becoming less capable of increasing its reimbursement to hospitals, physicians, and other providers. This dynamic will continue to shift responsibility from the commercial payers and government payers (to some extent), with the only alternative being taxpayers, including businesses. The financially well-off (i.e., those capable of paying a larger part of their total net worth in healthcare costs) will bear the bulk of the costs.
4. **Patients/Customers.** So, where do patients fit into this equation going forward? As stated above, those who can afford to pay more will do so through rising costs, offsetting the cost of care for those who cannot afford to pay. Patients must continue to become better educated about wellness. In addition, the early diagnosis and treatment of illness will, it is hoped, decrease costs.
5. **Employers.** Employers will continue to bear a greater portion of the costs on behalf of their employees, while asking their employees to do the same. This will equate to employers and employees absorbing a greater percentage of the "pie" for the overall healthcare costs. Private insurance will continue with a strong lobby and will remain the greatest benefactor vis-à-vis profits and margins.

TRANSCENDING PERSPECTIVES INTO MODELS AND RELATIONSHIPS

We have presented various affiliation strategies without much commentary toward favoring any one model. Deciding what type of affiliation, with whom, and how the components of such will be assimilated is often an almost insurmountable task; many plans never come to fruition due to an inability to even define the most effective structure.

The best way to determine the proper affiliation model is to review the options, understand them from both sell-side and buy-side perspectives, and use expert advisory assistance to move the process along. The final determination may be that it is impossible to pursue the deal, given the challenges identified early on. Thus, education and understanding of affiliation models are basic requirements. Often, physicians delegate this level of understanding to their advisers or even other physicians within their group legal entity. Administrative management will help determine proper structures; however, the owners of the business should be the ones who determine the best alternatives for affiliation.

Within our discussions in earlier chapters, we have carefully considered the various players, from private equity (PE)-backed sponsors to merged physician groups, to hospitals and health systems, and indeed all other possible investor-type entities. We have given these relationships considerable attention. In conclusion, we simply reiterate the need to follow the processes we have outlined.

FUTURE OF HEALTHCARE IN AMERICA

Now, let us consider the various components relevant to all affiliation transactions. These components can be opportunities as well as obstacles to completing an affiliation transaction. They consider the nuances within our healthcare industry and general business and investor environments, and affect every component of both buy-side and sell-side perspectives. As we break them down in the following list, we recognize that although we cover major areas, the list is incomplete.

Buy-side and Sell-side Perspectives

1. *Continued technological advances.*
   Healthcare and technology go together. Much of today's improved health outcomes are due to sophisticated technology, including imaging, surgical procedures, and other facets of care. While technology can be costly, it often inherently reduces the total cost of care. We expect such advances to continue.
2. *Emphasis on quality.*
   With technology and smarter, more efficient ways to deliver care (such as AI), quality will always be at the forefront of care provision.

3. ***Patient-first attitude.***
   While economics and return on investment will continue to be important, the attitude that the patient comes first, regardless of their ability to pay, will prevail. As discussed earlier, this will require some cost-sharing, including reallocation of resources from the "haves" to the "have-nots."
4. ***Academic excellence.***
   Much of the research, technology development, and other improved facets of healthcare emanate from academic institutions. Again, these resources require funding and will not bend, but potentially expand the cost curve, at least initially.
5. ***Attracting the brightest minds.***
   Many healthcare providers have no interest in their children becoming providers like them. The dedication of years and financial sacrifice will continue to be a major challenge in the U.S. healthcare industry. Enabling fair and commensurate compensation to physicians and other providers will help attract people to the profession, along with greater consideration of quality-of-life factors. When a bright individual can make significantly more money as an investment banker than as a physician, many will choose the former.
6. ***AI application.***
   The jury is still out on how much influence AI will have in the healthcare industry. Still, the brightest minds will prevail as surgeons and other specialists evaluate its use. Yet, AI is here to stay and will only become more pervasive.
7. ***Care coordination.***
   Clinical integration allows for such compliance and a view of restraint of trade, but our care is disjointed and lacks full functionality. Notable exceptions include large clinics such as Mayo, Cleveland, and others that provide the full continuum of care and thus have extremely effective coordination. In these organizations, the "right hand" knows what the "left hand" is doing. This is not always the case outside of such entities. Nonetheless, through technology, affiliation strategies, and other matters, our coordination of care will improve and not be overlooked. Such should indeed bend the cost curve.
8. ***Provider alliances.***

These will continue to grow from limited to moderate to full forms. AI, technology, and coordination of care will all contribute. An overarching theme of this book is built around affiliation strategies that "work." Such alliances offer real, sustainable solutions.

9. ***Payer-provider partnering.***
   In the past, the mere thought of payers and providers working together would have been impossible. Over time, payers and providers have worked together to find the best alternatives. We view this as a continued positive, and it will grow accordingly. That does not mean that providers must become payers, and payers must become providers, though this is okay if the parties agree. (See Chapter 10 for more extensive discussion of payer efforts to complete affiliation transactions and their nature.)
10. ***Government involvement.***
   Regulations, stipulations, checks, and balances, all within affiliation strategies, will be prominent going forward. Depending on the political party in control, these could vary widely, allowing flexibility in certain areas. Nonetheless, regulatory compliance will remain prominent, regardless of politics.
11. ***Aging population.***
   This is a major obstacle and concern for our healthcare industry. We want everyone to live as long as possible. We do not want to hinder the quality of life or the length of life in any way. Healthcare is about healing, and it always should be. Our population is aging, and the longer we live, the greater the utilization of healthcare and the resultant costs. Medicare and Medicaid programs are meant to help older people and those who are less affluent. We want them to weather the storms. But the system is challenged to be financially viable, and this will continue. Technology, cost efficiency, etc., are all necessary and must be developed. However, coordination of care and sound decision-making in patient care are even more needed. An aging population places greater stress on younger citizens, shifting the risks and responsibilities.
12. ***Greater demand for healthcare.***
   All the things discussed above are in play. Greater net demand will continue. Access to healthcare is essential, but depending upon the

point of view, it may or may not be an obligation of other citizens and/or the government. Government is nothing more than a representation of its citizens. As we become more aware of providers' ability to successfully treat diseases, we will want access to the same, regardless of cost. Who will provide this? That is the ultimate question. Aligning and integrating providers and payers should mitigate this.

13. ***Telemedicine and other non-patient contact processes of care.***
    COVID-19 opened the door like never before. It never would have brought telemedicine and related treatment processes to the level of receptivity without the pandemic. While the door remains open, most citizens prefer to go to their healthcare provider directly. But with an aging population and other stresses, including a significant shortage of providers in rural areas, telemedicine must continue to grow and serve as a viable form of care (which, in fact, it already is).
14. ***Economic opportunities and stress on all providers, payers, and the populace.***
    The things we noted above are a reality. They must be discussed carefully and fairly and divided among those taking direct and indirect responsibility for professional and clinical care. The cost and financial ramifications entail a great undertaking and will determine how our healthcare industry functions over the next generations.
15. ***Consolidation.***
    This book and its predecessor are about one thing: consolidation. Coming together, whether legally or informally, to render the best possible care for the lowest possible cost, and yet, the availability of financial opportunities will require continued consolidation. Hospitals and health systems will continue to employ physicians and APPs; PE will continue to look for opportunities to acquire healthcare services, including medical practices; clinically integrated networks (CINs) will continue to be formed; and groups will continue to merge to take advantage of that inevitable goal of "strength in numbers."

SUMMARY

So, there you have it! Our review of physician affiliation strategies is complete. Did we answer all the questions? Probably not. Did we provide some updated information, strategies, and overall goals and objectives for addressing our nation's great healthcare system? We hope so. We look forward to the next generation of healing and healthcare in the United States.

www.ingramcontent.com/pod-product-compliance
Lightning Source LLC
Chambersburg PA
CBHW071447230926
51846CB00001B/374
9781960762597